AUTHORITY

Authority

A Christian interpretation
of the psychological evolution
of authority

JACK DOMINIAN

Darton, Longman and Todd
London

First published in Great Britain by
Burns & Oates Ltd 1976

New edition published in 1981 by Darton, Longman and Todd Ltd
89 Lillie Road, London SW6 1UD

© Jack Dominian 1975, 1976

ISBN 0 232 51552 2

British Library Cataloguing in Publication Data

Dominian, Jack
  Authority.
  1. Authority
  I. Title
  261   BD209

  ISBN 0–232–51552–2

Printed in Great Britain by The Anchor Press Ltd and bound by
Wm Brendon & Son Ltd both of Tiptree, Essex

Contents

Introduction

Authority involves us all. We experience aspects of it in our family life, at school and throughout our education, in the church we belong to, and in the community in which we live and whose laws bind us together. Few subjects have greater interest — with the possible exception of sex. The meaning of authority and the way in which it is exercised actively concern all aspects of living.

The topic has won much attention in the last thirty years, since the end of World War II. It will probably be hotly debated for an indefinite period.

But this is no academic discussion. Attitudes to authority affect the ways in which parents and teachers behave towards children, and children respond to them; how citizens function in society; and the sort of society we want to live in. The Christian community is also a society, and in it believers apprehend the ultimate authority, which is God.

So widely-relevant and generally interesting a topic naturally evokes strong personal views. Almost everyone sets himself up as an expert in the areas in which he is actively engaged. Authority and discipline are topics on which everyone becomes an oracle, since how we act as parents, workers, teachers and leaders affects and makes continuous demands on the values and beliefs we hold.

At the same time, a particular section of the community — a group of professionals — has been emerging with a message that clamours for attention. They are practitioners of the psychological sciences: psychology, psychiatry, social psychology and so on. They often take part in the authority debate; either as interpreters of human activity or as healers of the ravages of too much or too little authority, they are actively involved in its many and ramified consequences.

Frequently, if not inevitably, there is a clash between these two groups of experts. On the one hand, all parents, teachers and individuals have the expertise of their own experience; on the other, trained persons bring to the discussion not only a wider perspective but the fruits of a growing body of research.

Encounters between the two groups can be illuminating. They can also result in those trained in the behavioural sciences shaking their heads in dismay over the stupidity of 'common sense', the weapon most frequently used by non-specialists, and the latter commenting with equal vehemence on the stupidity of all experts and the need to get rid of those who plague the earth with new-fangled ideas and belittle the value of authority, discipline and punishment. The personal habits of the 'experts', and in particular their children's lives, are scrutinized for any defects, so that when arguments run short of logic or persuasiveness, critical or abusive personal remarks take their place.

Despite the variable results of public debate, psychologists, social psychologists and psychiatrists occupy a large number of university posts, and are shaping the training of future teachers and graduates in many other subjects. Nowadays the medical and counselling professions pay more attention to human psychology and the significance of authority in human relationships.

This book is not an introductory text on one of the psychological sciences (although relevant references are given for all the topics discussed). It is an examination of *some* aspects of those sciences which are important in the relationship between personality, authority, and religion and the practice of religion.

My interest in the subject is rooted in daily clinical experience as a practising psychiatrist who also looks to the broader implications for the Christian faith as practised by individuals and in the wider setting of that community known as the Church.

To the familiar criticism that, by definition, a psychiatrist tends to be concerned only with extreme situations with no validity for the rest of society, I would reply that there is little evidence for rigid and distinct human characteristics dividing the 'normal' from the 'abnormal'. Instead there is evidence for quantitative characteristics or underlying universal traits. Everyone possesses a little of those traits, which are found in excess in behaviour treated by psychiatrists. It is not only possible but extremely instructive to study the characteristics of the abnormal, for they indicate the probable behaviour of all human beings under stress.

To use abnormality as a source of information regarding normality is perfectly legitimate, but it is not the only source of information I draw on. I also refer frequently to original psychological research. In the main this book is based on a combination of knowledge derived from psychological theory and clinical experience.

As in my other writings, the religious framework of reference is that of the faith in which I was raised and which I practise – namely,

Roman Catholicism — but the issues raised extend well beyond that particular denomination into the wider world of Christianity. They look forward to the day when once again Christians can pool their resources and energies to proclaim Christ in the style of their lives, in and through love.

Changes in authority and the Church

These are difficult days for all Christians but particularly for Roman Catholics. Until less than ten years ago, an average Catholic knew exactly where he stood with regard to his faith. Mass on Sundays was heard in a language totally foreign yet most familiar in sound. Participation included a minimal dialogue learned by heart from early childhood, and a series of movements: standing, kneeling and sitting with little variation, suitably dignified by a silence punctuated only by the ringing of bells at critical moments. This ritual was interrupted by the sermon, strongly influenced by a morality of rules and regulations and canon law. The Mass gave the man, woman or child who bothered to attend the essentials of a spiritual experience which confirmed closeness to God through a Church that championed authority, law, obedience, uninterrupted continuity and the security that accompanies clarity, certainty and minimal change.

And yet, apparently overnight, everything changed. Now bishops and priests spend a great deal of time and patience reassuring the faithful that nothing basic has been altered. The essentials of the liturgy are there; this is perfectly true but much has changed. The language, the dialogue, the involvement, the sequence and, above all, the nature of the sermon have changed, particularly when the priest is the product of the new theology with its emphasis on Scripture not canon law.

The few who are really content with the changes are those who have been helped to understand the background of theological change which influenced the Council.[1] These theological changes are still hardly grasped by the majority of lay people or priests; hence the confusion and puzzlement in the practice of the liturgy. Until understanding is far more widespread, the mixed uncertainty and apathy will continue.

But if a few prepared and determined theologians and bishops, who grasped the theological changes taking place for nearly a century, were able to influence the Council decisively (under the guidance of the Spirit), the Church at large was not similarly aware — in fact no one apart from a tiny minority was prepared and ready to consider the implications of change in areas other than the strictly theological.

1

One of the reasons for the gap between the hope and expectation aroused by the Council and the actual achievement so far (apart from strictly liturgical changes) is the poor preparation within the Church for understanding the changes in conceptualizing the nature of man that have occurred under the influence of sociological and psychological thought.

Once the new rule of open thinking was generally recognized, a clamour was heard, demanding the discussion of such topics as sexuality, contraception, celibacy, priesthood, child education and, to a lesser extent, the status of women, the rights of minorities, social justice, the aspirations of colonial countries and the appropriateness of fighting oppression in the name of justice (political, economic and social) with all available means, including violence.

At all these levels the Church, indeed Christianity as a whole, has shown a remarkable caution, not only because the topics are complex but because its inward resources in thought and preparation remain seriously behind its theological acumen. This is true of Protestantism and Roman Catholicism, and indeed all other major religious bodies.

A world fed on Darwin, Marx and Freud and other social scientists has become progressively concerned with the nature of man. Particularly after World War II the map of the world changed rapidly as nation after nation won independence from the authority and rule of colonial masters: from Britain, France, Holland and, finally, Portugal. This world-wide movement at the national level coincided with similar tendencies in groups and individuals striving for greater freedom at more personal levels.

The movement for woman's emancipation; the persistent efforts by students to have a greater say in the running of universities; the new militancy among junior doctors; all these joined other minority movements reflecting racial, sexual and ethnic aspirations for greater freedom, justice and equality. At a more personal level, the increase in outright rebellion by adolescents against their parents has brought the revolt against authority into the life of families left untouched by wider social and political movements.

In the end this relentless seeking of personal freedom reached the family. The amount of actual divorce reflects the refusal of individual men and women to yield to a life where their sense of personal dignity and happiness, as they perceive it, is being destroyed by the yoke of an impossible spouse. The family of priests and nuns has similarly witnessed an exodus of men and women who found their life too restrictive and inimical to personal dignity.

The massive social upheaval of our age, largely directed against the power of imperial nations and the authority of parents, teachers,

2

university professors, the state and so on, has involved the Christian Church as well.

The response of authority has been predictable and the answers inevitable. Those threatened by revolt have demanded the use of repression, reprisals, sanctions and punishment, political, economic, social, or physical. Sanctions and punishment are always advocated as the first appropriate corrective measure. But to be effective, these must have the backing of power. When the political and economic power that supported the colonial empires disappeared, those empires collapsed. The British Empire was dissolved with the least complication and bloodshed, and for that Britain deserves much credit.

The power of parents and teachers, and of all those in authority, has been similarly curtailed. This is no loss of political or economic power but a general change of opinion in a society which no longer upholds previous norms. Nevertheless the new autonomy is opposed by those who want a return to the past. There is continuous tension between those who want to increase individual independence and those who want to restore authoritarianism. Political experiments, of right- and left-wing governments, are made all over the world by democratic and non-democratic means. There is tension and conflict between those who advocate further advances in personal freedom and those who want greater control and greater exercise of authority. Communist and non-Communist countries alike are engaged in this struggle which involves personal standards and values. That is not to say that Communism or capitalism will refrain from using these human aspirations to further their own political ends if circumstances allow. But I do claim that civilization is faced with a personal growth of human consciousness affecting freedom and extending beyond political ideology and strategy, beyond plots and counterplots.

This movement towards greater freedom has caught the Catholic Church unprepared, not only because there has been no comparative study of the behavioural sciences to parallel the development of theology, but because the Church's basic system has depended so largely on a hierarchical system of authority, obedience and sanctions against rule-breakers.

These sanctions have relied hitherto on one basic principle which has had a long history and a wide Christian application: the fear of ultimate rejection by God in an eternity of hell. This hell has been garnished by a rich anthropomorphic projection of fire and torment and has certainly had a strong hold on man's imagination. But nowadays the fear of hell cannot intimidate or deter mankind. Even worse for Christianity, which has depended on mobilizing fear of external perdition as a motive for obedience and virtuous living, Christians

3

themselves will not accept such a picture of God. Christianity has no influence over its adherents other than the image of God that it proclaims. If that image no longer holds any terrors, then Christian practice can no longer be based primarily on threats of the consequences of neglecting or opposing such a God.

This change of attitude has taken place in those who still believe in God and hold the Christian faith. Needless to say, this fear-based religion has no meaning whatsoever for all those who claim they no longer need God to fulfil their lives.

The Catholic Church also has to face in its adherents a general trend away from a fear-based religion. But in addition to this widespread evolution, it has its own peculiar problem to solve, namely a transformation of its specific system of the practice of faith, based largely on rules, regulations and the sanctions attached to their violation. A faith based on and practised so extensively by canon law and principle received a violent jolt when overnight, after Vatican II, the emphasis placed hitherto on law suddenly shifted to a theology based on scripture, community and love.

These words were certainly part of the vocabulary of the Church but, if bishops, priests, or laymen were asked about the fundamentals of the practice of the faith, the majority would have emphasized the prescriptive details and the practical consequences of guilt and fear consequent to their violation. It is for historians to examine and evaluate the advantages and damage of such a framework of practising the faith. It is only too easy to criticize the system. It should be remembered that the Church of the recent past has had not only critics but admirers.

Whatever the shortcomings of the authoritarian framework of the Church, it provided clarity, security, order and unambiguous goals. The practising Catholic was judged to be a 'good' Catholic by attending Mass on Sundays and holydays of obligation, going to confession and communion at regular intervals, paying heed to the instructions of the hierarchy, marrying within the Church and sending his children to Catholic schools. Such a Catholic was assured within certain limits of 'salvation', and that was and remains the precious spiritual pinnacle for a Christian.

Only now, when the impact of scientific humanism[2, 3] has permeated all western societies sufficiently, is the traditional goal of spiritual salvation challenged by an alternative: human salvation in terms of raising man's freedom, dignity and fulfilment on the social and material levels.

Any penetrating examination of the gospels and the life of Christ shows that there is no basic incompatibility between these two. Much so-called left-wing Christianity is inspired precisely by the example, ideals and life of Jesus Christ.

This kind of tension between what are claimed to be the genuine goals of Christianity and the false, collectively-labelled 'middle class', or bourgeois standards and aspirations with which institutional Christianity of all denominations has associated itself, is stressed in the open rebellion against authority of the young and not-so-young.

But it is not my intention to examine in detail such social and political motives. Instead, my basic aim in this book is to assert that, whatever temporary fluctuations may occur in realization, the twentieth century is witnessing a new personal awareness of the meaning of freedom at all levels. From the macrocosmic and global level of national independence to the microcosmic level of seeking personal freedom as an expression of one's age, sex, race, social class or role as a single person, husband, wife, child, adolescent, worker, citizen, or of one's belief and faith, men and women are experiencing and asserting a new degree of personal consciousness. That new awareness will bring about different relations between those in and those under authority. This applies to all relationships: in the family, at school, at work, in society and in the Church. Christians have a fundamental responsibility not only to pay the most minute attention to such a change but to formulate a distinctively Christian view based on only one source: the life of the founder, Jesus Christ, as portrayed in the gospels and interpreted in tradition.

Such an answer will not be formulated easily or quickly since it requires fundamental changes in the structure of the Church. That is only too obvious in the Catholic Church but the Protestant Churches are no less obliged to work at this problem. In an excellent article on "Authority and the Christian Tradition", Professor Dunstan says: 'Nevertheless something must be said of the mediaeval and Reformation periods, for the generalizations commonly made about them — describing the first as an age of authority and the second as one, in reaction, of the individual — are both mistaken. There was an increasingly authoritarian element in the mediaeval Western Church as the central government extended control over doctrinal discussion as well as over the administration of canon law. But, in these terms, the Reformation was as authoritarian as the age before it. Authority was simply transferred, either to the Prince, as in England and Germany, or to an oligarchy of elders, as in the Calvinist Churches; and both could be as tyrannical as any pope or curia.'[4]

Over four hundred years have elapsed since the period described by Professor Dunstan and much has happened to the Catholic Church and the various traditions of the Reformation but I think it would be fair to say that, whereas the former certainly became more authoritarian —

particularly in this century — the rigidity of authority has remained in many of the reformed Churches, even if its form is distinctively different from the Catholic variety. Both divisions of the Church of God have to seek a different appreciation of man's aspirations, bringing to this challenge the experience and wisdom of their different traditions.

My own contribution will be in the narrow field of the development of the human personality from the psychological point of view. In all discussion of personal freedom there are two dimensions that have constantly to be considered and examined in relationship to one another. The first is the change brought about by the alterations in the environment which influence man. These are scientific, social and political changes. The second is the growing expansion of man's range of capacities as his physical and psychological capabilities are better understood. This book is primarily concerned with the second: namely our increasing insight into the natural development of the human personality, and hence the appropriate education, support and encouragement it needs to realize its full potential. Since parents and teachers play such an important part in this process, the role of authority and freedom in human growth is vital, particularly as it affects the early years of life which are now seen increasingly as vital determinants for the future of the personality.

Before examining this aspect of the growth of the human personality, I shall look more closely at some of the characteristics of current attitudes towards authority which are the targets of special criticism. In the next chapter I examine the psychological distinction between authority and authoritarianism, and in chapter 3 some of the dangers and limitations of obedience.

NOTES

1   SCHOOF, M. (1970) *Breakthrough* (Logos Books, Gill & MacMillan).
2   CONCILIUM (1966) *Church and World* (Vol.6, No.1)
3   CONCILIUM (1972) *The God Question* (Vol.6, No.8)
4   DUNSTAN, G.R. (1971) "Authority and Personality in Christian Tradition" in *Personality and Science,* ed. I.T. Ramsey & R. Porter (Churchill Livingstone, Edinburgh & London).

Authority and authoritarianism

If this were an academic treatise on authority, much attention would have to be given to the sources of authority in society, to the various powers exercised, and to the sanctions available. Authority, power and sanctions are the triad governing the relationship between those who enjoy these characteristics and those on whom they are exercised

The growing person experiences first of all the authority of parents or, depending on custom, relatives. Those *in loco parentis,* principally teachers, continue to exercise this authority, and ultimately everyone is subject to the laws of the State. There is, of course, a distinction between the legislative, judiciary and police functions of a State, and the balance of rights between citizen and State is one of the features with which the contemporary world is very much preoccupied. Even more important for those who prize freedom is the means by which power is obtained, whether by left- or right-wing governments, the crucial point being whether the people on whom this power is exercised have freely consented by democratic election to the particular form of government.

Christianity claims that all authority comes ultimately from God and the various denominations insist on the right to legislate for their own members in matters affecting faith and morals. The Catholic Church certainly heads the list of those with an extensive framework of canon law which describes in detail the necessary conditions for fulfilling the prescriptions of the Church.

It was at this point that Vatican II and subsequent developments raised many crucial issues. The Council itself made many advances in understanding the nature of the Church and made a considerable and inevitable shift towards a redistribution of power within it. The subsequent struggle has taken several forms.

First of all there is the crucial issue of the structure and balance of authority, and the polarization between those who want to safeguard the central authority of the Pope and the curia (and to ensure that in the balance of power between pope and bishops the former retains, as far as possible, his absolute independence) and those who favour

7

much greater interdependence.

The same battle of balance is to be seen all the way down the Church, between bishops and priests, priests and people. The outcome of this dialogue is far from complete. The arguments will continue for a long time about the degree of consultation between any two parties, but particularly the pope and others, the method of selection of the episcopate, their limits of power, the forms of sanction, the means of ensuring justice in any argument between two parties and so on.

In all this discussion several psychological issues are of the greatest importance, two of which are of such significance that they need to be fully stressed. The first one is that this struggle for authority and power can only have meaning if there is a readiness on the part of the ordinary man, woman and child to enter into the community and abide by its rules. One can be left with a body which has only leaders and no followers; increasingly, ordinary Christians of all denominations — and this now includes Catholics — are able to claim the fulness of being a Christian without joining the institutional organization, through fear or a sense of compulsory obligation. There is a growing sense of freedom and choice of terms on which an individual will enter and maintain attachment to any Christian body as the public (social) and private (guilt) pressures for membership and conformity diminish.

Increasingly, therefore, there is a need to examine the various struggles inside the Church between those members who are still used to the old structures and an ever-growing mass of younger people who find they want to join a Christian community with entirely different characteristics: a community that is concerned much less with authority and power and much more with service and love.

This theme of power and authority on the one hand and service and love on the other remains central in any future discussion about the nature of the Church and brings in the second vital psychological issue, namely the conditions in the community which encourage the expression of love. The next chapter will be largely devoted to this issue, which I examine briefly here.

For a large part of this century the Catholic Church has relied on a code of canon law which has regulated much of the life of its adherents. The training for the priesthood consisted of philosophy and theology and a substantial part of the latter was really an extended course of canon law. This is not surprising, for a great many of the everyday decisions affecting the practice of Catholic life were related to canon law directives. Canon lawyers were much sought after and a combination of such training with further orthodoxy instilled in a Roman seminary were not infrequent ingredients for promotion to the status of bishop. No one can deny that law had an all-pervasive impact on the

Catholic community. In the short time since Vatican II the memory of this is already beginning to fade as other theological priorities begin to assert themselves, but the issue is far from dead. Commissions to bring canon law up-to-date are in existence and there are many theologians who would be horrified or lost with a Church that did not have a canon law system. This is not the place to argue the vexed question of whether an up-to-date canon law is required or not. Quite clearly the existing one has been so extensively superseded by conciliar decisions that basic alterations are inevitable.

What is beyond argument is the following psychological point. Whereas it is perfectly true that a clear and precise law brings order and clarity, removes ambiguity and sets definite limits to what is and what is not required or permissible, a Church that relies primarily on a system of law has little relationship to the basic tenets of love.

All our loving experiences are learned in the bosom of our family where the signals and behaviour of recognition, acceptance, care, tenderness, affection, conflict, forgiveness and separation are *personally* mediated. All the rules and regulations that existed in our home were in fact subordinate to a person-to-person, intimate, intensely personal interaction between ourselves and our parents.

When rules and regulations are detached from a personal bond, they become part of a system which regulates the association and conduct of individuals in any institution which needs order, coherence and stability for its functioning but does not assume or encourage close personal ties between its members. Law detached from intimate personal encounter becomes an impersonal instrument for effecting order and justice and operates in all organizations which are large enough to lose any sense of intimacy and personal meaning.

The contradiction of the Catholic Church was that it was a body that modelled itself on the family; the Church was called mother, the priest father, the pope Holy Father, its nuns sisters, non-ordained religious brothers, and yet its life was largely regulated by a canon law system and practice much more befitting a large organization in which impersonality was the key feature.

This impersonality permeated right through the Church in the marked social and emotional distance that separated the pope from his bishops, bishops from their priests, priests from their flock and members of religious communities from each other. The spontaneity, intimacy, and closeness of family life were replaced ultimately by the distance and impersonality of canon law.

Of course few actually recognized this in such bold terms. Much went on at a personal level and behind the scenes which by-passed the harshest strictures of the law. Able casuistry and personal care allowed the demonstration of love. The defenders of the past would also remind us of the effort spent in caring for orphans, the destitute, the sick and the poor. This is true but counts for little because it is implicit and obligatory in the life of the Christian community. Furthermore, the handicapped and the destitute form only a minority, albeit a vital one. What matters a great deal more is the practical life of the Church in its sacraments, such as marriage, which impinge so basically on the life of the majority: the rigidity encountered here, particularly in the cases of mixed marriages, with the massive disapproval shown by the Church, coupled with a minimal flexibility when marriages broke down, stemmed from a background that placed law at the centre and love at the periphery. That was also frequently seen in the advice and spiritual help given in which priests certainly made themselves available fully but always within a framework that imposed severe restraints. Frequently dialogue broke down simply because there was no dialogue. The Church made the pronouncements and that was the end of the discussion.

Many of those reading these sentences will perhaps take issue with me on this matter. Surely no pope, bishop or priest should alter the law of God or Church for the sake of individual needs.

The law of God was, of course, a phrase that relied heavily on inflexible and rigid natural law principles which had not made enough allowances for the fulness of love. These principles operate much less nowadays because there is a greater understanding about natural law[5] and the availability of a theology based on scripture and love. Frequently the issues that bothered the ordinary Catholic were those concerned with sex problems, marriage, mixed marriages, education of children and the consequences of marital breakdown. Here, as is increasingly recognized nowadays, the weakness of the theology of sexuality and marriage was at its most marked and the law of God, sincerely believed, was nevertheless an inadequate substitute based on legal requirements.

The post-Vatican II Church must ensure that this order never repeats itself, not only because it is the wrong order for any Christian community but because there is a basic inconsistency in any community that should be aiming to foster love yet relies on law as its main instrument for promoting this love.

That is not to say that rules and regulations have no place. Of course they have, when they are clearly seen to be no obstacle to the social and emotional interaction that love demands, nor to hinder its growth, which ultimately depends on the continuous development of the personality.

The failure of growth of the personality, which is the main issue treated in this book, means that thinking, feeling and action are controlled through fear, anxiety and therefore result in narrow, limited and protective behaviour. How damaging this consequence can be is demonstrated by one of the classical studies of social psychology of the last thirty years, which introduces the subject of the authoritarian personality.

Authoritarian personality

Some who have read this book so far may already have made up their minds that I am opposed to authority and law and therefore either a dangerous liberal or an extreme left-wing anarchist. Others will probably expect me to declare that all authority is really an expensive and unnecessary luxury in society and that we would be much happier with less law, discipline and punishment.

I must disappoint both because I do believe that authority and law are an inescapable part of human life, whereas I am at the same time committed to the view that, however necessary both are, they can never be the principal means through which life is sustained. The significant distinction however is between the person who is exercising and obeying authority and the authoritarian personality.

What is meant by the authoritarian personality? Certainly not someone who is exercising authority, but someone who approaches his own authority and that of others in a particular way and who also tends to have certain other characteristics which together form a distinctive and easily recognisable personality.

The research which has led to the famous book *The Authoritarian Personality*[6] arose from a conference of the American Jewish Committee held in 1944 which considered religious and racial prejudice. The sufferings of the Jewish community in Germany and Europe under the Nazi occupation were clearly a determining influence on such research. Ultimately the research workers constructed an 'F' scale, F standing for the Fascist personality. On the basis of extensive research the results pointed to a combination of features that identified the prejudiced, authoritarian person with the characteristics of the Fascist personality.

Such a person is one who, in addition to the tendency to be racially prejudiced and ethnocentric — 'feels secure when he has his niche within a social hierarchy, who is submissive to those above him and dictatorial to those below him. . . . respectful and subservient towards authority, brusque and rather contemptuous towards his subordinates, repressive of his own instincts, conservative and convention-bound in his beliefs, generally opposed to licence and self-indulgence and in favour of discipline, and punitive and unsympathetic, towards "sinners", particularly if they are judged "inferior" in some way'.[7]

The description of the authoritarian personality was one of the

11

landmarks of research in social psychology. The original publication is a lengthy document but a briefer form can be found in a collection of important documents of sociological interest,[8] which also contains the scientific critique that has been levelled against the study. Nevertheless, despite its defects, the formulation of the authoritarian personality has withstood most of the onslaught for many reasons, not least of which because it is an easily recognisable description of many people who, without necessarily depicting all the features, exhibit enough to form a cluster of traits that are to be found in individuals in all walks of life.

This personality has particular significance in any situation where the ideology of a system or organization tends to encourage the ideas of authority and discipline, emphasizing the dangers of sex and applying severe punishment for all violations and especially to those who seek sexual self-indulgence and who dare to stand up and criticize lawful authority. It does not require much imagination to see that Christianity as popularly conceived and misinterpreted by its most zealous and misguided adherents would include in its ranks such authoritarian personalities. Whether such ardent advocates of Christianity belong to the hot-gospeller variety or the sophisticated intellectual version, they use Christ as a symbol to support just about everything that would have been repudiated as a proper Christian attitude by the originator of that faith.

Since some aspects of the authoritarian personality, such as respect for law, avoidance of destructive self-indulgence and hard work can be shared by many others, the possible confusion and danger when the extreme form of the authoritarian personality speaks on behalf of the Christian faith is obvious.

One point about the authoritarian personality which needs emphasizing is that, as it stands in the original research, such a person tends to be right-wing and conservative. Nevertheless, the intense rigidity which is associated with such a personality is certainly not confined to conservatives. Those who hold left-wing political views may not be prejudiced about racial issues but may have strong nationalistic tendencies and hold equally strong and inflexible views on other matters, as for example the attitude of certain student organizations about freedom of speech for certain speakers considered to be politically on the right. The authoritarian personality may be found in any ideological system. Dogmatism is not a prerogative of any political party.

Open and closed minds

Closely related to the findings about the authoritarian personality is another study which has examined the nature of dogmatism. Rokeah's research has led to a description of the open or closed mind as it relates to the belief system held by the individual. [9a, b]

There is a belief-disbelief dimension held by each person reflecting first of all the *isolation* between the two. Thus the principles of Christian love, understanding and forgiveness, honesty and truth which are sincerely expressed on Sunday may be completely isolated from the beliefs practised a few hours later at home or next day in a cut-throat, competitive business world. An extension of this isolation is the likelihood of *contradiction*. Thus, war, aggression and brutality may be fervently declared to be bad and evil and with the same breath, if one is a Jew one may say they are justified against Arabs; or if one is a Catholic in Northern Ireland, these same means are justified against Protestants, and *vice versa*. Christians are frequently attacked for preaching love and justifying wars and other cruelties in the name of their faith, but such contradiction is certainly not confined to them. One further feature of isolation is the *exaggeration* of *differences* between belief and disbelief.

In pre-ecumenical days all Christians, but particularly Catholics, were only too aware of the black and white pictures that were painted of Catholics and Protestants and the frequency with which such distinctions were made and even preached from the pulpit. The exaggeration of difference is not a Christian prerogative but an everyday experience when there is need to oppose for the sake of opposing; or to convince without sufficient supporting evidence. In addition to isolation, contradiction and exaggeration of differences, belief and disbelief are governed by the degree of differentiation between two different systems. The well-differentiated system of belief allows the believer as much information as possible regarding those matters which he accepts and those he disbelieves and rejects. Absence of such differentation often means that the rejected system is treated with certainty and conviction regarding his unworthiness without sometimes any knowledge at all, or sufficient knowledge, to judge the comparative merits of the two systems compared.

These qualities of isolation, contradiction, exaggeration and differentiation provide the basis for a distinction between the open and closed mind. The closed mind maximizes all these characteristics and holds firm, strong, unchanging, unyielding views which admit of no ambiguity, doubt or change.

The open mind on the other hand is exactly the opposite. It is always open to change and development in the presence of justifying evidence for such alteration.

Open and closed minds are to be found in a variety of degrees in all spheres of life and not least in the Christian community in all its denominations. The closed mind of the Catholic against any other religion was, of course, virtually the official teaching of the Church which altered somewhat in the statement of Vatican II: 'On the other hand, Catholics must joyfully acknowledge and esteem the truly Christian endowments from our common heritage which are to be found among our separated brethren. It is right and salutary to recognise the riches of Christ and virtuous work in the lives of others who are bearing witness to Christ, sometimes even to the shedding of their blood.'[10] This is certainly the foundation of a most welcome ecumenism, which is so essential for the urgently-needed renewal of all Christianity.

What are the factors that contribute to the authoritarian personality or the closed mind? It can be stated categorically that, whatever the reasons, they are certainly multiple and are not specifically related to religion as such, for these characteristics can be found in the personalities of any believer or non-believer in God. If the remarks in this chapter appear harsh towards some Christians, it should be said in all fairness to Christianity that those who contemptuously dismiss all Christianity as authoritarian and those who find it impossible to comprehend how anyone can remain a Christian and retain an open mind are both mistaken. There are plenty of Christians who are both open-minded and non-authoritarian; many non-Christians — indeed non-believers — exhibit all the features of the opposite. Certainly a close examination of the life and behaviour of Jesus Christ, who came to confirm not to deny the law, nevertheless will find great difficulty in discovering any traits of intolerance, prejudice or lack of openness. In fact, his tolerance for all, his attacks on conventionality and the rigorism of the law, the self-righteous, the unyielding, the oppressive, those who uphold the letter and not the spirit of the law were the accumulative indictments that brought him to his death.

But can we draw closer to the reasons that produce the rigid, closed, authoritarian person? Research does not provide any detailed information but clinical observation gives us some hints. Frequently such a man or woman is more than averagely anxious. This anxiety leads to insecurity which requires the most powerful and effective protection. This protection is to be found in authority which in turn supplies the basis of certainty and guarantees immunity from all personal weakness and uncertainty. Those in authority are then treated with awe and respect for they become in some way the source of life for the individual who feels at the edge of a personal precipice. He fears disintegration if left to his own resources. What authority claims, states, demands is sacrosanct and woe to the one who criticizes it, for in criticizing authority he is threatening the very foundations of this person's belief and existence. Hence this belief must be protected by being isolated, insulated, safeguarded. The other person *must* be wrong or else *I am finished*. The system which I believe *must* be right or else something dreadful will befall me . . . I dare not look too closely in case I am confronted with the possibility of a total loss of confidence in my identity; if the beliefs I have surrounded myself with are taken away I am left naked and empty and liable to be overwhelmed with the panic and anxiety of nothingness. . . .

Perhaps when all this applies to the Christian faith, it is most appropriate to remind ourselves of the words of Our Lord — 'Oh ye of little faith. . . .' Those who protest most loudly at any change, who are fearful lest authority should lose its invincible status, should ask themselves whether they really do have faith in the Christ who proclaimed that the 'gates of hell shall not prevail . . .' It is not authority *per se* that forms the Church but the totality of its members who proclaim Jesus Christ as the Son of God. Authority of course must play a part in preserving and teaching the truth; but it is a truth which is continually unfolding and to hold to it in an ossified way is no service to Christianity.

NOTES

5   FUCHS, J. (1965) *Natural Law — a theological approach* (Dublin, Gill)

6   ADORNO *et al* (1969) *The Authoritarian Personality* (New York, W.W. Norton)

7   WRIGHT, D. (1971) *The Psychology of Moral Behaviour* (London, Penguin), p. 188

8   MADGE, J. (1970) *The Origins of Scientific Sociology* (London, Tavistock Publications), p. 377

9a   ROKEAH, M. (1960) *The Open and Closed Mind* (New York, Basic Books)

9b   ROKEAH, M. (1968) *Beliefs, Attitudes and Values* (San Francisco, Jossey-Bass)

10   VATICAN II *Documents* (1965) (London, Chapman), p. 349

The dangers of obedience and conformity

The last chapter described some of the dangers of authority. I turn now to some of the attendant risks of obedience. Christianity has extolled the virtues of obedience to legitimate authority and the Catholic Church has made obedience a cornerstone of its practice. And yet clearly there are many dangers in obedience, particularly blind obedience, which require proper emphasis if the subject is to find the perspective it deserves. This chapter deals with the inner world of those who commit acts of violence on others under the compulsion˙ of obedience. And since the passage of time reduces the horror of devastating events I draw my example from a holocaust of recent history.

There must have been hundreds, thousands, if not tens of thousands, of individuals involved in administering the extermination of Jews in Europe in the last war. When finally they were brought to justice, most of them pleaded as an excuse that they were obeying orders. On the surface most of them were ordinary people who would have been horrified to inflict violence on their neighbour but obedience converted their spontaneous disinclination to do so into a series of actions which form one of the most appalling crimes in the history of mankind. Similarly, obedience unloaded the bombs on German and British targets, and the atom bombs on Japan; obedience produced extermination policies in the Vietnam war from South Vietnamese combatants and their American allies, as well as similar inclinations in the North Vietnamese.

Those who want to read an eye-witness account by one of the American soldiers who took part in the horrifying My Lai massacre in Vietnam can read it in the New York Times of November 25th 1969. This comment reveals no political bias, I have no doubt that appalling massacres were perpetrated by Communist forces. The risk of destroying life, property and goods in the name of obedience is not confined to any political ideology; the common denominator is an act of obedience to authority.

Most people would agree that all such practices are regrettable but necessary during a war. After all a country's future is at stake and military discipline and obedience are vital if the State is to be preserved. This answer is obviously inapplicable to the extermination of the Jews, questionable to say the least about the American involvement in Vietnam, and equally questionable in many other minor exterminating or punitive expeditions which occur continuously throughout the world.

What would be claimed with sincere conviction is that the infliction of undeserved and unnecessary pain in its extreme form could never occur in ordinary, civilian life. And such a belief would be seriously mistaken, as the brilliant experiments of Stanley Milgram[11] have shown. Those who really want to acquaint themselves with a modern experimental research of outstanding psychological merit can do no better than read Milgram's study which presents no difficulty in understanding even to the non-specialist.

The experiments were carried out in the Interaction Laboratory of Yale University, USA. The aim of the research was to find out the limits of obedience in a situation which involved inflicting pain on another human being. The experiment was so arranged that there were three people involved. The first was called the 'teacher', the second the 'learner' and the third the 'instructor'. Of these three only the first was unaware of the conditions of the experiment. He or she was in fact the average man or woman in the street whose reaction was being assessed. The 'teacher' came to the laboratories freely in answer to an advertisement requiring help with experiments in learning and memory. The experiment consisted of a contrived situation in which the 'teacher' read out a pair of words such as blue box; nice day; wild duck and then a sequence of words like sky, work, box, lamps and the learner was required to associate correctly one of these terms with the first word announced. If the answer was wrong he was punished by an 'electric shock' administered to the wrist. The 'teacher' was placed in one room, with the 'instructor' and the 'learner' in another. In front of the 'teacher' was a board with a number of switches measured from 1 to 30 shock levels representing 15 to 450 volts i.e. increments of 15 volts at a time. Each time the 'learner' made a mistake the shock level was upped to the next stage.

In fact there was no electric shock, the 'learner' was always the same person who was a member of the experimental team and so was the 'instructor'. But the 'teacher' knew nothing of this. He or she proceeded as if the pain inflicted was real and the reality was made more convincing by the simulation of pain on the part of the 'learner' from faint complaint to the most violent and blood-curdling screaming, pleading to be released from the strapped position whilst the 'instructor' demanded that the experiment should continue.

Under these conditions how were the subjects expected to behave?

17

Here the reader may draw upon his own views and make his predictions. A number of people were asked before the experiments for their own .predictions, which are summarized as follows: A number of psychiatrists, graduate students, undergraduates and middle class adults were asked how the 'teachers' would behave in these experiments. They predicted that almost all subjects (teachers) would refuse to obey the experimenter (instructor). These conclusions were made on the assumption that people are by and large decent and do not readily hurt the innocent, unless bullied by physical threats or coercion and that decisions of this nature are made from the depths of the individual who freely assesses the consequences and acts accordingly.

In fact 26 out of 40 subjects obeyed the orders of the experimenter to the end, continuing to punish the 'learner' in the continuous presence of painful, yelling, screaming and agitated behaviour, because the experimenter instructed them to do so, even though they were administering shocks of extreme intensity (as they believed) to a helpless victim (as they believed the learner to be). In a variation of the experiment the 'teacher' was first told that the 'learner' was suffering from a heart condition but this made little difference to the outcome.

In case it is thought that these 'teachers' were particularly callous, insensitive people, their behaviour showed that they were not because they all experienced and expressed conflict and tension. In fact it is the continuation of their punitive activity in the presence of this marked conflict stress that betrays the powerful hold that authority and obedience have over us.

Changes in the experimental conditions produced marked alteration of behaviour. First of all the physical proximity of 'teacher' and 'learner' was altered. If the learner was brought closer by placing him first in the adjacent room and then in the actual room itself, the number of 'teachers' who withdrew earlier from their punitive activity increased.

The relationship between physical proximity and the pursuit of damaging behaviour is vital in modern society. Increasingly man is able to produce weapons with unprecedented lethal consequences which are manipulated at a distance from the victim. When we attack another person physically, the consequences of hurting them are visible and have an immediate impact. But the bullets of guns strike at a distance, bombs are dropped from planes, atomic weapons can be projected from planes, submarines and ships. All this places a distance between aggressor and victim which diminishes any personal encounter and so reduces the safety or braking margin of emotion and therefore compassion.

The same applies to the administration of law in a complex

bureaucratic society in which human beings become numbers on a file and the file assumes an impersonality which no longer draws a personal response from the person administering justice or executing a course of action. Innumerable clerks must have been responsible for the planning and completion of the concentration camps and gas chambers and for arranging transport for the victims. Involved with a small part of the operation or handling a person for a transient period with total absence of personal interaction diminished the chances that sympathy, care, compassion, affection would be an intervening factor.

A combination of blind obedience, rigid application of law and impersonality are a most dangerous triad which contemporary society has to guard against as industrialization encourages the growth of amorphous, human complexes.

Some of the revolt within the Catholic Church reflects a certain amount of this precise combination. Criticism of what has happened is useful but, even more important for the future of Christianity, if it is to act as an important social influence, it must order its own internal life in a way that will become a model for the world, showing how to handle destructive forces in a way that minimizes the potential dangers and enhances the growth of love. *There is no doubt that in any renewal of Christian influence this objective must assume a high priority.*

To return to our experiment: The physical presence of the 'learner' acted as a brake to the continuation of the punishment but the physical absence of the 'instructor', the source of authority, also acted as a brake when, for example, he left the room and/or gave instructions by phone.

Dilution of the influence of authority also came from the presence of more than one 'teacher'. In another variation of the experiment, instead of having one 'teacher' there were three in the room, the other two also being members of the experimental team. Each in turn refused to obey the 'instructor' and withdrew. Under these circumstances the 'teacher' found it easier to withdraw from the experiment.

Everybody knows it is much easier to confront authority in the presence of others rather than in isolation. Numbers add strength and every school, home, army or state recognises the strength of opposition when rebels combine to oppose. The principle of ruling by dividing the opposition is a common one and the effective answer is one for all and all for one, such a successful measure in strikes.

Some surprise may be shown that there was no difference in the outcome between men and women. Women would be expected to be more sympathetic but, on the other hand, are in general more co-operative in tests of compliance. In practice women showed the same level of obedience as men but experienced more conflict in the process.

All the 'teachers' were in fact interviewed afterwards and told of all the details of the experiments, including the faking of the victims' reactions. There was little evidence that the 'teachers' knew what was going on, which gave greater assurance of the reliability of the results but, of course, this reliability depended much more on the actual observations of the 'teachers' behaviour during the experiment, which confirmed the agonizing reality of the situation for them.

Milgram examines these results at some length. The propensity for obedience is present in all of us and is shaped at home and school. We enter readily into hierarchical structures in which authority defines appropriate action. As soon as such an obedience stance is accepted, one of the vital consequences for the person is that responsibility is felt towards those authorizing the action not for the content of action, and much emphasis is placed therefore on loyalty, duty and discipline. For this reason actions carried out under command tend to absolve the victim from responsibility in the sense that responsibility is seen to lie with authority which is interpreted as knowledgeable and intelligent, unlikely to demand improper behaviour. Furthermore, when a person enters a situation of obedience and accepts authority, he enters into a binding relationship which is difficult to break without questioning the competence, status and wisdom of authority, all of which creates anxiety, fear, embarrassment and inner doubt. A great deal of courage and determination is required to defy authority which has previously been accepted and obeyed.

Disobedience in these circumstances is so difficult that a sequence of events is required in which the subject first experiences inner doubt, then external doubt, then disagreement and threatens disobedience before the final break occurs.

Milgram sums up his position as follows: 'Consider an individual who, in everyday life, is gentle and kind. Even in moments of anger he does not strike out against those who have frustrated him. Feeling that he must spank a mischievous child, he finds the task distasteful: indeed, the very musculature in his arms becomes paralyzed, and he abandons the task. Yet, when taken into military service he is ordered to drop bombs on people, and he does so. The act does not originate in his own motive system and it is not checked by the inhibitory forces of his internal psychological system. In growing up, the normal individual has learned to check the expression of aggressive impulses. But the culture has failed, almost entirely, in inculcating internal controls on actions that have their origin in authority. For this reason, the latter constitutes a far greater danger to human survival.'[12]

Perhaps the point that culture has failed to inculcate internal controls on actions that have their origin in authority is exaggerated. Without them rebellions would not occur, corrective measures would not be taken, whereas in practice they are. But the general statement is absolutely true that obedience is infinitely the greater force than disobedience.

The advantages for humanity so far have been obvious. It can only survive by acting together under the guidance of leaders. This can be seen in animal species and, indeed, it is seen in many human situations today. An army *does* need obedience, rules have to be followed on the highway, on the sea, in the air or else we die. Most authority is wise and benevolent and is obeyed with advantage at home, school and in society. But obedience is not without its dangers, particularly as men's capacity to destroy each other escalates with the advances of technology. It is becoming increasingly clear that, in addition to obedience, mankind must arm itself with a greater capacity for evaluating authority. The capacity to assess is necessary not only because authority is clearly not always right, but because the consequences of it being wrong are potentially far more destructive in the contemporary world.

Perhaps the general move towards challenging authority at home, school and in society may be the beginning of a corrective measure but it is too early to say whether this is in fact the correct interpretation. Disobedience *per se* is no virtue unless it challenges views, opinions, actions, orders which are incorrect and dangerous. What is advocated in this book is not a move towards anomie, anarchy or disobedience for its own sake but a much greater balance between obedience and *autonomy*. There are no advantages in social or emotional chaos. Those who fear these consequences as an immediate outcome of changing human behaviour can be reassured for obedience to authority is a deeply rooted human characteristic. A far greater risk at present in the world is the likelihood that one authority will be replaced by another, whether it is politically of the extreme right or left. What is needed is a raising of man's autonomous capacity to act as a self-directing person who can evaluate the claims of all authority. *Christian claims to educate and foster the moral man must make this another priority.*

Conformity

A close relative to obedience is conformity. Both obedience and conformity demand a certain amount of reduction of personal initiative and the acceptance of direction from an external source. This external source is usually a parent, a teacher or figure of authority but it is often as much an action of compliance as that of imitation. We do what others do, not necessarily because they have asked us to. Examples of conformity as an expression of imitation abound in everyday life — the formation of a spontaneous queue is a ubiquitous example, the gathering of a crowd to watch upwards in the direction of a plane or building, downwards into a hole, the little child who joins behind a marching group, the joining in community singing and myriads of other examples.

Conformity is not of course anything like as dangerous as obedience in the context of the present discussion. The person conforming has a sense of freedom and choice which is not present in the subject under obedience and therefore he can withdraw with much greater ease. But there are other dangers far more subtle which need stressing.

Conformity may be a solitary action. We, as individuals, copy others in behaviour involving only ourselves. But frequently conformity is a social group phenomenon. It is in this situation that special risks arise. In group situations a distinction has to be made between social and interhuman or inter-personal reaction, a distinction made by Buber.[13] The inter-personal is the encounter between two persons. The social demands a suppression of individual interaction in favour of group activity which frequently, but not necessarily, pays attention to conforming activities of a collective nature. A group comes together to accomplish a common purpose agreed by its members. This may be to watch a game of football, play bingo, listen to a lecture or music, carry out a piece of work or project, pray or live together in an organization. Inevitably the emphasis in a group is in shared, social action with marked emphasis on conformity, thus individuality is damaging to group coherence.

A great deal of research has gone into the dynamics of groups but this is not the subject of discussion here. What is of interest is the danger of conformity. Let us take as an example the practice of the life of the Catholic. Sunday Mass is certainly a group activity. Before Vatican II, the practising Catholic came to a church with many other men, women and children and entered into a ritual whose details were indelibly registered in his personality. Conformity played an enormous part. On entering the church he made the sign of the cross with holy water, genuflected and then knelt in prayer before sitting down. When the bell was rung the priest entered with the altar servers and a series of actions followed which consisted of kneeling, standing, sitting, kneeling, standing, walking to communion rail, retiring from communion, kneeling and possibly sitting, kneeling, standing and walking out. The verbal sequence in a strange language was known by heart and the *Dominus Vobiscum* brought a conditioned response *(Et cum spiritu tuo)* in the best Pavlovian manner. The sequence of conformity was broken in the sermon, except that frequently the opening sentence would be a signal for a sermon virtually known by heart.

Here is a situation which maximizes the social encounter and minimizes the interpersonal. The interpersonal is of course meant to be between man *and* God, for here is the central liturgical event of the worshipping activity and the ritual is meant to enhance this.

But the Mass is primarily an interpersonal encounter and therefore, if the social process of conformity denies access to the interpersonal, then the experience is fraught with dangers.

In fairness to the Church, this point is certainly appreciated but the emphasis on physical attendance at Mass, at confession and communion, which are considered to be the criteria by which the Catholic has been assessed as practising and 'good', are clearly extremely dangerous criteria unless the social situations of Mass and communion in particular are also occasions of interpersonal encounter between man and God.

It is at this level that one aspect of the argument has taken place between those who favour the old Latin Mass and those who want the new English form. The new form is of course still a ritual, a social grouping with all the attendant dangers of social interaction instead of personal encounter. The vernacular brings the participants into closer ties, although English can still become a conditioned sound activity, just as much as the Latin. The kiss of peace certainly attempts to bring that interhuman encounter with our neighbour which the Mass should inspire. And yet what a difficulty this kiss of peace has been in so many places, demonstrating the whole point of this subject, for here the social group breaks down and becomes for a moment a series of personal, interhuman encounters.

We look at the man or woman next to us, behind us, in front of us. We smile, we recognize them perhaps for the first time, we touch them, we may even, if we are bold enough, kiss or embrace them. Our first experiences of being human occured in the arms of our mother when we were held, touched, kissed, hugged and we reciprocated by smiling, babbling, looking, touching, feeling close to her. The kiss of peace is of course much more than a symbol of peace; it is a brief but powerful human encounter.

It is a reminder that the encounter with God in the Mass must have its counterpart in the encounter with man, not only at that moment but the next and the one after and the day after. In fact, every minute of the day we must remain in personal, human encounter with our neighbour in a process of love, if we are to be truly Christian.

This contrast between the social group activity and the interhuman can also be seen in other situations as for example in religious life or at school. Nuns and monks get up and pray together, they eat (or used to) together, pray and sing together. All this and much else was done *together*. Everybody conformed and much attention was paid to punctuality, the appropriate action (amount of time spent kneeling, contemplating, listening to approved reading) and so on. Yet this group activity took place against a background that did not encourage, in fact discouraged, the truly interhuman. In so far as closeness encouraged personal relationships, the result was considered as dangerous, particularly if intimacy assumed the character of being a 'special relationship.' As in the Mass, the personal was avoided and social group activity encouraged. At school similarly there were innumerable group occasions for prayers, attendance at Mass and other liturgical events with massive pressures to conform by attendance.

Now, in the name of heaven, someone will ask, what is the complaint about? Surely human beings need social groupings, ritual and common activity. They do indeed, but the advantages of the communal and social are only completed in the presence of the interhuman, one without the other is simply incompatible and fosters one of the greatest dangers for all Christians, namely *pseudo-mutuality*. God cannot be cheated by ignoring each other, nor can he be reached without active awareness in and through love of our neighbour. On the surface everything appears to be all right. People come to church, go to Catholic schools, enter religious life, pray together, attend pilgrimages, protest about abortion in thousands. All this gives a semblance of mutuality, of reciprocal encounter between man and God and man and man. But only if this expression of faith is translated truly into love in the daily encounter between two people can the mutuality cease to be pseudo-mutuality, and for this to occur the accent must be on an awareness of the other.

Hence the emphasis in recent times on involving members of the community in various activities at Mass, such as reading, taking the bread and wine to the altar, participating in the kiss of peace; and on the need for much greater interpersonal encounter at school, in the convent, in the monastry and at parish level.

Both obedience and social conformity are necessary, and ritual activity is a vital part of daily life, but their effectiveness is only complete if the experience is translated into the interhuman encounter of love. No one watching Christianity today can fail to see that one of the vital steps it must take is to shift the emphasis from obedience and conformity to autonomy and the personal encounter, for both make far stronger demands of love and no amount of preaching about love will be effective unless human beings are taught to recognize and translate it into action every moment of their lives. Only when Christians are seen once more doing this in sufficiently recognisable terms will the world take notice of them again.

NOTES

11   MILGRAM, S. (1974) *Obedience to Authority* (London, Tavistock
          Publications)
12   Ref. 11: p.147
13   BUBER, M. (1965) *The Knowledge of Man* (London, George Allen & Unwin

24

The origins of conscience

Introduction

In the previous chapters I used such words as authority, dependence, independence, anxiety, guilt, punishment. The foundations of all these experiences are laid in childhood and particularly in the first dozen years or so.

Looking at the advances that the behavioural sciences of sociology and psychology have made in the last seventy-five years, there will be little argument that a detailed examination of childhood has been one of its major contributions. Our knowledge is still sketchy and undoubtedly much will be added in the future. But at the present moment there are three original and different theories about human growth, all of which have marked relevance to the subject of authority and obedience.

These will be treated separately in the next three sections. The first one owes its origin to Freud who emphasized the role of instincts and emotions. The second comes from Piaget who did not pay a great deal of attention to feelings and emotions but directed attention to the cognitive or thought development of the child as well as to his moral growth. Freud and Piaget described theories which were developmental in nature, in the sense that every child is conceived as following a sequence of phases, each of which builds on the previous level of achievement. Each phase has its own characteristics and lays the foundations for the next. Maturity is conceived as the successful and effective handling of the issues raised by each phase and is seen as progressive mastery and integration. Thus immaturity is the exhibition of behaviour which is appropriate for an earlier stage of development than the chronological age of the person. Every individual has to master the physical, social, emotional and moral requirements of growth and one of the features seen frequently in adults is a marked incongruity between various accomplishments. The retarded adult shows normal growth physically but inadequate intellectual development. It is far more difficult to see the disparity between normal or even unusual intellectual achievement coupled with emotional immaturity. Frequently the psychiatrist has the responsibility of helping to bridge the gap. The disparity between moral growth and the other dimensions is not infrequently seen in courts but has a much wider impact on society.

In addition to the theories of Freud and Piaget there is the school of behaviourism, which has no single originator but is indebted to all learning-theory advocates, such as R.R. Sears.[14] Basically, this theory relies on the principle that all behaviour is either facilitated and reinforced or discouraged and eliminated, depending on the consequences. Pleasurable consequences strengthen a response, painful ones weaken it. Learning theory does not postulate any particular series of stages of development. We are continuously in the process of learning or unlearning particular sequences of behaviour.

Basically, all three theories make valid contributions and must be seen as a whole, but for the sake of clarity I shall treat them separately.

I Freudian theory

In this section I give an outline of Freudian theory and then rely largely on Erikson's extension and modification of it.

Freud drew extensive theoretical conclusions about the development of the human personality from his clinical data. That one person could construct such an extensive theory from such meagre resources and yet revolutionize human thought is a measure of his genius. Much of his underlying theoretical framework is seriously questioned nowadays, particularly his revolutionary emphasis on sexual energy as the foundation of growth of the personality. But his attention to childhood, its significance for later life, the role and importance of the unconscious, the importance of instincts, the means of defending ourselves against anxiety by conscious and unconscious 'defences', and the use of psychoanalysis as an original therapeutic procedure, have stood the test of time.

The human personality is considered to depend on the outcome of the development of two basic instincts: *libido* (or sexual energy) and *aggression*. Between them these two instincts mobilize the basic energy of the growing child and three key sites of the body are the main channels through which this energy is discharged. The first is the mouth, the oral, the first of the nominated erotogenic zones. With the mouth the child first experiences the pleasure of sucking, chewing and masticating; and with the mouth it discharges its first aggression by biting its mother's breast. The mouth remains an important source of pleasurable activity, such as eating and kissing through life.

The oral phase is negotiated in the first year of life. The second and third years shift instinctual attention to the other end of the body, the anus, where elimination takes place. Defecation is not only a source of satisfaction to the child but a major social achievement in the area of order and cleanliness. Success also brings conflict between the wishes of the mother and those of the baby for whom its mother's requirements do not initially make sense. Frustration, conflict and battles of will may follow, and toilet training can become an emotional battleground.

Inevitably the anal phase will be negotiated; the child learns bowel control, and concurrently – or soon afterwards – the third and final, the phallic or genital is reached. Much of Freud's psychology was male-orientated. Hence the penis becomes the centre of libidinal attention. The boy at this stage not only becomes aware of his penis but experiences a specific anxiety, the fear of its loss or castration anxiety. He compares his body with that of the little girl who has no penis or perhaps has lost it. But how?

Here Freud's theory enters its most complex construction. The little boy is in fact considered to be attracted towards his mother, wants to possess her and possess her exclusively. But father intrudes menacingly. Father is powerful and potentially punitive, hence the worst fear that is likely to befall of course is the loss of the penis, if not in reality, then certainly in phantasy. This dreaded event must not happen. The little boy gradually learns to give up any of his desires for mother, abandons any hope of displacing father and gives up his jealousy in this triangular situation. The oedipus complex is resolved. The fear of castration recedes. The boy now gets closer to his father, in fact he begins to identify with his male characteristics and the phallic phase is negotiated. And for Freud that is the end of the road. The successful resolution of the oedipus complex means the successful resolution of the instinctually based development of the personality. Thereafter a so-called latent period follows until puberty brings about the physical sexual awakening which does no more than make it possible to proceed with heterosexual attraction already achieved through the male identification with father in the resolution of the oedipus conflict.

In addition to this libido development, Freud postulated a mental structure which he called id, ego and super-ego. These were hypothetical structures which have no real anatomical, physiological or other somatic counterparts. But the id is the part of the mental apparatus with which the child is born. It is composed of the unorganized, pleasure seeking, instinctual forces seeking discharge with no sense of direction or control. The id is said to be unconscious and operates on hedonistic principles; the pleasure principle governs its operations. However, as the child begins to grow, he becomes aware of another dimension, the presence of mother, father, brother, sister and others. These people satisfy their wishes and demands on the child. The child is no longer free to indulge in uninhibited pleasure seeking because some of this is forbidden, disapproved of, or simply not available. This is the world of the possible and available and impossible and unavailable, the world of reality, and the ego has now charge of this phase. The ego acts as guardian between the presence of the id, seeking pleasure and the world of reality, of what is possible. There is frequently tension between the id and the ego and some of this may be unconscious. Finally, there is a third element of the mental structure, the super-ego. The child learns what the parents approve and disapprove of and this knowledge extends to other significant figures whose standards, edicts and rules now become part of its world of regulations. They are gradually internalised. The standards of the adults get inside the child, producing anxiety and guilt when transgression occurs. Such guilt feelings need not arise in the visible presence of the adults. The adult is carried inside symbolically and may remain there for the rest of life, acting as a watchdog. The super-ego is often compared to another word which describes similar but not identical characteristics, namely conscience. Here are Freud's own words about the super-ego: 'Psychoanalysis has been reproached time after time with ignoring the higher, moral, supra-personal side of human nature. The reproach is doubly unjust, both historically and methodologically. . . . But now that we have embarked upon this analysis of the ego we can give an answer to all those whose moral sense has been shocked and who have complained that there must surely be a higher nature in man. "Very true," we can say, "and here we have that higher nature, in this ego ideal or super-ego, the representative of our relation to our parents. When we were little children we knew these higher natures, we admired and joined them; and later took them into ourselves."[15]

Psychiatrists have often to deal with what the priest might call a scrupulous or sensitive conscience but they describe as a severe super-ego in Freudian terms. That is to say they have to treat a person who is constantly on his guard in case he has broken some rule, displeased or offended someone, failed to do something, not only unimportant but also trivial, has a tendency to check and re-check his behaviour for its defects, feels excessively guilty over any real or imaginary misconduct and is particularly sensitive about disobeying anyone in authority, particularly his parents. Such guilt feelings lead to the need for punishment and reparations which are often well in excess of what is justified by the misdemeanour. Frequently such a person is really responding to an excessive anxiety which is easily and unnecessarily aroused and it is this anxiety that needs reducing. The feelings of guilt over trivialities are particularly distressing but their very intensity betrays their pathological source which is due to the marked anxious make-up of the individual rather than to the measure of his badness. The obsessional personality is frequently to be found in the clinics of psychiatrists and may seek solace from the clergy as well.

The simplicity of a single agency responsible for all censuring and guilt producing behaviour is very attractive and the concept of conscience or super-ego is a most useful one. But whereas both describe a force within us which is responsible for the peculiar quality of anxiety, called guilt, it is unlikely that all moral violations are organized by the single entity which Freud called super-ego or that conscience is more than a convenient term describing a much richer array of human responses.

Erikson, who follows the Freudian psycho-analytical line carefully but has enriched it, expands the concept of super-ego into a much broader range of experiences. He remains faithful to the vital significance of feelings, emotions and instincts which are described according to the dynamic theories of growth. But these are no longer confined to the two instincts of sexuality and aggression, although these occupy a prominent position.

The development of personality according to E. H. Erikson ([16]a,b)
Essential to Erikson's thinking is the belief that the child goes through a sequence of developmental possibilities which are either fully realised and adequately responded to by the parents, thus facilitating mature growth, or the opposite. In practice the process of maturation is always a mixture of the various possibilities. Erikson sees growth in terms of specific crisis periods, which give the child the 'sense of', the feeling of particular emotional quality which subsequently is built into the life structure of the growing person. Each crisis phase has a polarity; there is the positive and negative experience and the predominant feeling is the result of the interaction with parents and adults which is then carried through to the next phase. Since the majority of children remain with their parents throughout childhood, the conspicuous traits of the parents will become the features that are widespread in the personality of the growing person.

Such a description emphasizes the influence of the environment, in the form of the parents. But clearly this is only one of the determining factors. The make-up of the child, its genetic inheritance, will be the other influential factor making it more or less resistant to an adverse influence, more or less co-operative with any advantageous one.

All growth proceeds in this interaction between the inherited resources and the environmental influences. This explains how children may grow up to be markedly different from each other even though they are brought up by the same parents.

The sense of trust versus mistrust

The first year of life is defined as the one which gives the child a sense of basic trust. It is a year in which the continuation of life is utterly dependent on the presence and care of mother or mother-substitute. The child cannot look after itself. It is fed, held, changed, moved, bathed. In all this there is a marked passivity and dependence. The point that Erikson stresses is not only the obvious one that without food, warmth, protection and care the child will perish, but that given these are adequately supplied, what really matters is the quality of the exchange which is primarily physical. At this stage the interaction is dominated by sound, and particularly by looks and touch. The baby cries and the mother picks it up. The baby cries and the mother appears. There is face to face contact which continues at feeding time and the sense of trust begins to develop, depending on the signals that are interchanged. Does the mother respond with a smile? with interest? But of course, most important of all is the quality of touch in the way the baby is handled.

Perhaps there is no more convincing example of the disparity between a sense of trust and mistrust than to consider the case of a battered baby.[17] During the last couple of decades increasing attention has been paid to the arrival of young babies in casualty departments of hospitals and elsewhere who, on examination and particularly an X-ray, are found to be bruised and to have multiple fractures of their bones, the undoubted result of violence by the child's mother or father. This evidence is often the result of throwing the baby physically on the floor or across the room or lashing out with fists and hands on its delicate body. This is not the place to consider the circumstances which give rise to such a situation but it illustrates the contrast between a child being picked up with care, given the feeling of being held securely in the mother's arms, hugged, caressed and kissed, and being thrown violently on a bed. The sense of trust and mistrust learned through physical experience is here exposed at its most extreme contrast.

The sense of trust conveyed by physical encounter through seeing, hearing and touching another person remains one of the fundamental aspects of security throughout life and has a particular relevance (hardly understood yet outside scientific circles) in sexual activity. Even in these circles far too much emphasis is placed on the pleasurable aspects of sexual intercourse, neglecting the fact that the intimacy of sexual intercourse is the adult equivalent of the recurrent closeness experienced by baby and mother. Sexual incompatibility is not only a loss of sexual pleasure but an even much greater loss of the means of fostering a sense of trust.

The other experience of significance in this first year is the child's receptive — or in more Freudian terms, oral — incorporation. Everything is being done to the child, whose first year is a combination of passivity and receptivity, with an emphasis on receiving through the mouth but this is extended to a wider setting of its whole body which is receiving the attention of touch. Dependence is thus a matter of *receiving* from others and in its earliest inception this is a type of experience about which the child has no choice. If the way it receives experiences essential for survival is unpleasant or painful, two things can be set in operation. The first is to associate closeness and receiving with such unpleasantness that behaviour in the opposite direction is set in motion. The child begins to withdraw from something distasteful. Of course it may withdraw because of its make up, which does not find physical contact with another person satisfying, but what is emphasized here is the beginning of withdrawal from others in the form of finding receptivity and acceptance difficult. This withdrawal may become an increasingly active process in the course of development and the speed and ease with which we withdraw from other human beings depends not only on the rapidity with which we experience mistrust but also on the level of freedom and independence which society permits in terminating personal relationships.

The greater freedom to terminate situations which cause a sense of mistrust in international, national and personal relationships is a feature of contemporary society and is seen most clearly in personal relationships between parents and children, children and teachers, adults and lecturers, employers and employees, husbands and wives. This freedom runs contrary to the hitherto prevailing principles of loyalty, duty and the obligation to tolerate a much greater degree of discomfort in relationships, particularly with those in authority from whom withdrawal was a reluctant and rare event.

Autonomy versus shame and doubt
The second and third year of life are extremely important ones in the child's development. This is the time in which standing, crawling, climbing, walking are accomplished. Feeding goes through the mess familiar to every mother with the hit and miss process of spoon being guided to the mouth and accompanying mess on the face and table and floor but with the ultimate gradual success. To locomotion and feeding is added the unique human acquisition of speech and, of lesser significance, the capacity to dress oneself. It will be remembered that

Freud stressed the anal phase during these years: that is, the child's capacity to learn about retention and elimination in its bowel control. But the child advances in much more than bowel control as it plunges into a world of gradual autonomy and here, for the first time, the human personality enters the world of personal freedom.

In the process of acquiring the skills of autonomy the child is bound to be involved in difficulties. While clearly programmed to acquire these functions and keen to achieve them, with the possible exception of a rigid bowel training regime, how much the child will be allowed to experiment, that is to say the pace, encouragement and help for achievement, will of course depend on the parents.

All this learning is carried out on the basis of trial and error. The spoon hits or misses the mouth at the start of feeding. The vest is put on back to front, the right shoe on the left foot, and the consequences of crawling, standing, climbing are hilarious and possibly expensive if breakable objects are left around. Even more important for the child's safety, the need to put medicines beyond reach is vital. All this learning requires patience and encouragement from parents and needs a great deal of time.

There is also inevitably a good deal of frustration on both sides; conflict, aggression and, not infrequently, the odd smack. Here then is the first crucial stage of independence or autonomy versus control.

The mother can in fact do many things for the child, thus retarding progress through overprotection. She can allow the child to experiment without help and lay the foundations of neglect. She can shout, scream, punish and the child can be stubborn, scream and defy in return. But at this stage of life defeat for the toddler is inevitable; the opposing forces are totally unequal.

Much more commonly, autonomy proceeds with a mixture of facilitation, encouragement and frustration. But the quality of the interaction is vital. Is the mother praising sufficiently each moment of success? Life during these years is a constant opportunity for Nobel prize victories. The moment of successfully putting on a sock can feel and be treated as a resounding success or treated with frustration and despair. Does the mother praise or does she underline the helplessness and incompetence of the child, constantly taking over and retarding progress? These are the years which foster, in Erikson's words, *self-control without loss of self-esteem* and 'From a sense of self-control without loss of self-esteem comes a lasting sense of autonomy and pride; from a sense of muscular and anal impotence, of loss of self-control, and of parental overcontrol comes a lasting sense of doubt and shame.'

This is what he has to say about shame. 'Shame supposes that one is completely exposed and conscious of being looked at — in a word, self conscious. One is visible and not ready to be visible; that is why we dream of shame as a situation in which we are stared at in a condition of incomplete dress, in night attire, "with one's pants down." Shame is easily expressed in an impulse to bury one's face, or to sink right then and there into the ground.'

Christian thought is familiar with the first parents' desire to hide from God's sight after the act of disobedience (which provided such a valuable text for antisexual propaganda when Adam's sin was somehow interpreted as a sexual one). Long before sexual activity occurs, we all experience ourselves in the process of mastering a new technique under the gaze of others, and the sense of accomplishment or failure is a recurrent feeling which goes on throughout life as we acquire new skills and feel appropriately ashamed or proud of our achievement.

Those who are extremely suspicious of all talk about greater freedom and interpret it as an invitation for the abandonment of all control and direction should note the absurdity of such fear. The second and third year in life is a model for all learning situations. The process of acquiring new skills requires advice, help, encouragement and the setting of limits, of rules and regulations if the child is not to damage itself. Rules and regulations remain essential throughout our lives as a means of protecting ourselves and society but they are instruments of fostering order for development, not the means of perpetuating control over others.

Too little control means chaos and loss of the appropriate conditions of growth, too much control not only means retardation of development, but also fosters an increase in shame, doubt and uncertainty and these can become enduring characteristics of the personality.

However, just as in the first phase attention was drawn to inherited characteristics that militate against the ease of achieving physical closeness, so there may be factors which militate against autonomy. The speed with which physical control is acquired depends on co-ordination, space, vision and time perspectives, the speed with which frustration is mobilized and also the anxiety that is felt in opposing mother or father. All these and other features vary between one child and another and govern progress in autonomy. It is the optimum interaction between the child's needs and the parental response which is the key to optimum growth in this and all subsequent stages. This interaction must have the right balance between control and freedom, encouragement and disapproval, reward and punishment. Those who advocate excess of one or the other are invariably pursuing ideologies and ignoring reality and, in so far as Christianity has tended to favour the ideology of excessive control, it must seriously re-evaluate its position because it is certainly wrong. In doing this there is no need to turn to the opposite and abandon all sense of direction or control. The key is a graduated interaction.

Initiative versus guilt

Freud placed the core of guilt feelings in the oedipal situation reaching its climax in the fifth and sixth year. Boy wants mother but cannot have her because of father, girl wants father but cannot have him because of mother. This is one of the central theoretical Freudian concepts, and the resolution of oedipal, triangular situations relieves the acute guilt feelings by abandoning the forbidden instinctual wishes. Erikson certainly goes along with the sexual aspects of the fourth, fifth and sixth years of life but extends the basis of guilt.

Having acquired a considerable range of new functions, the child begins to explore *what kind* of a person he is going to be and the model he wants to imitate is that of the parents. He wants to be like them but the gap between his aspirations and his achievements is considerable and his failures are associated with guilt feelings.

This newly discovered world without limits is investigated by the intrusive mode. Intrusion includes 'intrusion into other bodies by physical attack; the intrusion into other people's ears and minds by aggressive talking; the intrusion into space by vigorous locomotion; the intrusion into the unknown by consuming curiosity' and, of course, the sexual intrusion of the oedipal phantasy of wishing to displace the parent of the same sex and take over his role. 'For those sinister oedipal wishes (so simply and so trustingly expressed in the boy's assurance that he will marry mother and make her proud of him and in the girl's that she will marry father and take much better care of him) in consequence of vastly increased imagination and, as it were, the intoxication of increased locomotor powers, seem to lead to secret phantasies of terrifying proportions. The consequence is a deep sense of guilt. . .'

For those who simply cannot accept the sexual origin of guilt feelings, Erikson will not be any more convincing here than Freud except that for both guilt encompasses the feeling of violating parental wishes and prohibitions in the development of the super-ego and every parent recognises the mounting and accumulating occasions for saying 'no' and punishing the child of this age group whose frontiers of autonomous behaviour are rapidly extending.

All Freudian theory attempts to explain a subsidiary but important feature of guilt in some people, namely the excessive degree of guilt feelings which bear no relation to their behaviour or the severity of parental discipline and punishment. Some adults claim to feel extremely guilt-ridden from this age onwards and careful assessment of their childhood does not suggest excessive bad behaviour on their part or severity on the part of the parents. It is this gap between external reality which induces guilt feelings and internal experience which is theoretically accounted for by the child's inner world of dread due to its sexual phantasies.

But once again there are alternative explanations, such as for example the child's proneness to anxiety reaction. There is no doubt that some children are far more anxious than others and the psychiatric history of adults is filled with accounts of being excessively shy, easily frightened, finding it difficult to mix easily with other children, taking to heart parental disapproval far more intensely than was warranted. These same men and women go on to exhibit a far greater range of fear reaction in their adolescence and adult life and their excessive guilt feelings may be associated with the greater ease and persistence of anxiety reactions which are now related to a real or imaginary, but always exaggerated, sense of badness, following confrontation with or violation of authority's direction.

What Erikson stresses is the need to ensure that the relationship between parent and child during this phase and the next one of the school years exhibits an equality in worth despite differences in functions, capacities or chronologically related accomplishments. Here is an essential prerequisite for the breakdown of any future persistent inequality based on authoritarian relationships and the earlier this sense of personal value is transmitted to the child the easier future relationships of equality of personal worth will be established.

There are two other stages described in the child and adolescent phase but these do not primarily refer to the topic under consideration and will not be considered further.

II Cognitive theory

Cognitive theory, which owes its origin to the Swiss psychologist and research-worker Piaget, starts from a very different viewpoint to those of Freud and Erikson. Not feelings, but intellectual development is treated as the principal constituent for the development of personality. The faculty of knowing is the key to human growth, and here there is a theory which fits in with the traditional emphasis in the educational world on intelligence and intellect. But from what has already been described it can be seen that no theory of development can ever be complete by itself. Cognitive growth takes place concurrently with emotional development and to ignore one or the other mitigates against the concept of human wholeness. There is little doubt that this is precisely what has happened in western educational thought, which has excessively emphasized the intellectual against the emotional.

Cognitive development, like psycho-analytic theory, progresses by stages in which thinking acquires greater richness and complexity. For Piaget, doing and knowing are intimately related to produce cognitive human behaviour, which in turn depends on the physical maturation of the organism. Adaptation is the aim of the organism. The thinking person strives to establish a balance between himself and his environment, and this in turn depends on assimilation and accommodation. The organism assimilates, or in other words takes in, new experiences all the time; but what is taken in can only be integrated at the level at which it is experienced subjectively, and no further, however complicated it is. Piaget's richness of theory lies in a detailed description of how the child's assimilation enlarges as its relationship with the environment changes in the first twelve years or so. If assimilation is the subject's response to the environment, accommodation is the environment's impact on the subject. A piece of music may be interpreted simply as a pleasant noise but gradually, through accommodation, the detailed constituents of the noise, the full reality of the music, may be grasped. Now the individual not only assimilates but accommodates. For Piaget the constant aim of the organism is adaptation which is a balance between assimilation (what can be taken in depending on the subject's level of experience) and accommodation (the enlargement of experience in order to do further justice to the stimulus). This behaviour is a two-way exchange of action by the individual on the environment and the action of the environment on the individual. The basic unit of the cognitive structure is called a schema, which is an established pattern of a meaningful, repeatable psychological unit of intellectual behaviour or its prerequisites, which are continuously modified as a result of activity.

It is not the intention to describe here in any further detail the stages of development, the first year described as sensorimotor, the second to fourth years as preconceptual, the fourth to seventh years as intuitive, except to emphasize one vital feature, namely that until about seven or so, when the child reaches the stage of operational thought, its life is dominated by what Piaget calls egocentrism, a word of vital importance.

There is hardly any discussion on morality or ethical behaviour which sooner or later does not locate all human badness in man's selfishness, self-centredness, egoism. Psychiatrists are attacked because they are always trying to find excuses for people's unacceptable behaviour and their outlook is held responsible — at least in part — for the rising rate of antisocial behaviour. If only people stopped behaving selfishly, all would be well. Implicit in this statement is the assumption that, if they cannot control their egocentric behaviour, they should be restrained by punishment. The recurrent conclusion is that people need more discipline. There is just enough truth in all this to make it plausible in the usual superficial heated emotive discussion. And yet, despite the millions of times these conversations are held, apparently man becomes no less selfish or self-centred and is in fact unlikely to do so unless notice is taken of the emerging understanding of the nature of human growth, so that education adapts accordingly.

In the sense that Piaget used the word, 'egocentric' refers to the fact that the child experiences a confusion between itself and the external world. It is a confusion between the 'me' and the 'not me'. He is unable to conceive any perspective other than his own. 'He assumes that his understanding of a situation is *the* understanding of it. He thinks intuitively, and in images rather than concepts; he is unable to think about his thinking and discover his own inconsistencies and contradictions. Above all his thought is completely dominated by those features of the environment that he is perceiving or noticing at the time . . . in Piaget's term his thought is centred. Since he cannot liberate himself from immediate perception he is unable to compensate for the distortion that perception introduces in his judgements.'[18]

Egocentricity is certainly a feature of human behaviour in so far as the child is incapable of differentiating itself from others, a situation which gradually changes in childhood but never quite disappears, even in adult life. Particularly under conditions of stress, perception narrows down to the immediate, the concrete and the self. Any driver can recall how conversation with fellow passengers ceases and, indeed, their very existence ceases at moments of driving stress, e.g., in difficult motoring conditions. Under stress it is a common experience to concentrate on personal awareness and survival. This tendency to return to earlier forms of thinking and acting under stress is often responsible for placing the individual in the invidious position of appearing socially or morally insensitive to others. Normally we recognize the strain of driving and make allowances; sometimes the fast driver does not make allowances for the state of terror of those beside him! In fact daily life is full of moments when stress narrows our awareness of others and we return to an egocentric style of experience and action. The trouble is that neither the person nor the onlooker is aware of the reason for the change, which is interpreted as deliberate, with malevolent intention leading to one of those all too frequent human chains of interaction in which we know we have acted in an egocentric way, feel guilty by outward standards but in our heart of hearts we know we could not have behaved differently and feel there is an injustice in the criticism, which reinforces the feeling of not being understood.

Up to the age of seven or so the child does not have the means of freeing himself from egocentrism. Subsequently changes occur in his thinking and his awareness of others which make this possible. Thinking becomes operational which means that he is now capable of sufficient detachment between himself and his surrounding world, so that he realises that reality may be different from the way that motor, sensory, verbal and symbolic signals of perception suggest. From about seven to eleven or so, this operation is still dependent on concrete stimuli from the environment. Beyond this stage thinking becomes formal in the sense that abstract thought, which is no longer dependent on immediate sensation, is possible. This detachment from the immediate environment has parallel experiences in the world of moral development which needs to be considered next.

Up to the age of seven the child knows the world only as he sees, hears and touches it with his body, through words and appropriate signals. The result is that he expects everyone to understand him without having to explain himself. This unity between object, action and thought, which continues until the age of concrete operation, has a special application to obedience. Father, mother and figures of authority are objects whose rules and commands are absolute. Once their special position has been accepted, and this is virtually automatic for all children, obedience is blind and has no differentiating features. Obedience means being good and is absolute whilst disobedience is absolutely bad. There is no hierarchy of values. Everything is either good or bad. Breaking rules has also this simplicity. Intention does not come into the child's life in these early years. Everything is assessed by sheer quantity. The amount of lying, damaging, disobeying is what matters; the underlying reasons or extenuating circumstances are not considered.

Punishment follows closely on these beliefs and is proportional to the gravity of the misdeed, once again regardless of the underlying circumstances. The child expects automatic punishment as a form of *expiation* which accompanies immanent justice, that is to say it is the subject himself who delivers a verdict of guilty and expects punishment automatically every time he does something wrong.

Such is the morality of the young child; it is labelled moral realism by Piaget. Moral rules are external to the child, totally related to authority and punishment has to be literal, automatic and regardless of circumstances. Social relationships are of course totally dependent on parents and figures of authority towards whom there exists unilateral respect.

One can see that much of the obedience, discipline and punishment thinking of authoritarian figures relies on this early pattern of our lives. This is not surprising. It is one of our earliest experiences and we are therefore heavily conditioned to it. We return to it in all conditions of danger. The discipline of an army is very much like it and we accept it at times of disturbance or war. We drop into such automatic discipline and obedience at all times of danger such as those associated with accidents on motorways, outbreaks of dangerous disease or even in the phase of acute illness when we obey the orders of a nurse or doctor unquestioningly. In all these situations we abrogate our judgement, we hand ourselves over to others. Such a situation means that human beings can be managed with the least amount of interference from private judgement, decision or *reciprocity*.

Much valid criticism has been made of the hierarchy of the Catholic Church which ruled largely in this way until Vatican II. There were of course great advantages in this blind and automatic obedience to authority. What was not appreciated, however, was that the level of maturity present in such a response was appropriate to the early years of life and so the Church was in danger of being an organization which encouraged immaturity in its members. Both hierarchy and laity reinforced this emotional immaturity in each other.

Very often nowadays the hierarchy comes under severe criticism for its behaviour, but the laity is just as much at fault for allowing this situation to continue for so long. If there is to be blame it certainly does not belong in one place.

This moral realism changes into a morality of co-operation and reciprocity in the older child. With the growth in his capacity to think in terms of wholeness and not just parts, a sense of certainty develops as an intellectual operation can be accomplished from beginning to end and, if necessary, reversed back to its beginning. Children can order their experience, not independently of others but in relation to them. They see themselves as capable of independent thought, but now recognize that this is a process which others are capable of as well. Relationships of reciprocity with peers begin round about seven years or so, but may be later depending on the level of development of each child.

There is now a significant shift from unilateral respect hitherto addressed to parents and figures of authority to *mutual respect*. The child's capacity for independent thinking also means that he is aware of himself and others in a more autonomous manner. Rules cannot be changed arbitrarily and unilaterally. Agreements are mutual and have to be respected. This sense of equality which first appears with peers must inevitably extend to parents and figures of authority, a process which is well on the way by the end of the first decade of life.

Such a morality of co-operation, reciprocity or mutuality means that the punishment has to fit the crime, in the sense that justice becomes a reality in its own right and is gradually detached from authority *per se.* Justice and punishment are based on the assumption that equality, fairness and the possibility of reforming rather than expiation will set up the behavioural scene.[19]

The stage of development from unilateral to mutual respect, from a morality of realism to a morality of reciprocity is crucial for any discussion of faith, obedience and morality in the Christian community. It has of course a particular application for the Catholic faith.

In general the relationship to authority can either be encouraged to give way to a relationship of autonomy, mutuality and reciprocity or it can be encouraged on the basis of unilateral respect. There is little doubt that the latter often happened in the Catholic Church and particularly to figures of authority such as priests, bishops or Pope. In so far as this occurred, clearly it maintained a relationship in which both parties assumed less than their fulness of maturity in the relationship. But the implications are much wider than those that pertained in the Church before Vatican II.

Men and women can grow and develop a relationship of autonomous reciprocity with everyone except their parents, superiors, bosses, police and all figures of authority. There is a widespread movement amongst the young to bring such behaviour to an end. This is often mistaken as an attempt to break down order, to bring disrespect to authority and to destroy society. There is of course a danger in all social and moral change but the majority who wish to change the pattern of behaviour have no destructive intentions of the type ascribed to them. Authority retains respect in so far as it is legitimate and is used for the ends for which it has been ordained. It has no special privileges as such and it is certainly *not* sacrosanct.

This does *not* mean it should not be obeyed or respected in so far as it carries out the responsibilities allocated to it by the community but it has no implicit privileges in itself. A young child treats authority with absolute reverence and blind obedience until the age of seven or eight and then begins to evaluate others in reciprocal terms. This is the most useful process which ensures that authority can never become damaging by using its powers detrimentally.

There can be no doubt at all about the real and distinctive moral advance of the child if it is encouraged by the presence of parents who facilitate the transfer from unilateral to mutual respect. Erikson drew attention to the need of a parent to develop the sense of mutual worth in the presence of unequal capacity and achievement some two or three years before the cognitive development of the child can grasp the beginnings of this change.

If parents and teachers do not encourage the growth of mutual respect, they are encouraging the crisis of later adolescence in which young men and women have to attain their independence after leaving school but cannot do so because the appropriate autonomy and self reliance have not been encouraged.

Even worse, men and women of outstanding intellectual ability can develop remarkable talents in their work or business and be giants in their own right or, for that matter, just exhibit ordinary competence and yet retain an immature and obsequious attitude to authority.

In Catholic circles, the 'Yes father, no father' dialogue arising out of unilateral respect, extending right through the hierarchy, has perpetrated a system of relationship that is more befitting the nursery or primary school relationships. But one can see this elsewhere in life. The damage is twofold. Either authority is treated and encouraged to be omnipotent, which places an impossible burden on it in trying to fulfil this role, or people show this childlike respect towards authority figures before their faces and behave differently out of sight.

But since the Christian community is there to express the reality of the Church, the body of Christ, it is the damage to faith that matters most. In so far as faith was related to such unilateral respect and went no further, then it partially explains the massive withdrawal from the outward institutional Church. If authority has fallen into disrepute, then the faith that depended on unilateral respect has also disappeared. If the reality of God depends on maintaining such infantile structures of relationship then the demise of Christianity is comprehensible and fully-deserved.

But clearly the existence of God and the reality of Christ are challenges which extend well beyond the principle of unilateral respect towards authority and the teaching of faith must disengage itself completely from such dependence. Belief in God can survive only when the relationship with such reality progresses beyond unilateral respect and there is no future for Christianity unless this is fully accomplished.

Following Piaget's thinking, another worker, Kohlberg,[20] has advanced a more refined system of moral judgment. He described three levels each with two stages. The first level is described as premoral and its two stages are conformity to those who have power to punish and a second stage in which everything is justified which satisfies needs. There is no sense of personal responsibility to others. They are there simply to meet our needs. At the second level others do exist and their point of view has to be considered but, like Piaget's unilateral respect, the 'other' is very much 'authority' that has to be pleased and respected. The third level of morality is now a morality based on self-accepted principles which require that authority be opposed if these principles dictate it to be so. We are here at the level of reciprocity in which others have rights which should be respected but behaviour is morally autonomous. The last stage is an extension of this autonomy which can now conceptualise universal principles extending beyond the personal level.

Both Piaget's and Kohlberg's schemes are being subjected to rigorous testing experimentally with positive results. But the general development of morality from the prudential to the authoritarian, social and then personal is the finding of research of nearly fifty years ably reviewed in a recent book.[21]

Education has to revise extensively its ideas at this level if it is going to encourage mature development and this process of change is already taking place. But for obvious reasons, namely that all response to authority begins in its most elementary, blind and automatic form, we tend to return to that form under stress or uncertainty. It is the most deeply ingrained response and both society and religion have tended to rely heavily on this mode and to turn to this early level when they have been under attack or threat.

And yet any hope of really advancing human maturity must depend on encouraging the later levels of personal autonomy which are the very ones that produce the truly personal and human moral response. Traditional morality has always acknowledged the limiting effects of the presence of fear and coercion on free choice and responsibility. And yet it has held contradictory positions by, on the one hand, noting the diminution of responsibility in reality (a mortal sin was defined as the presence of serious matter with full knowledge to which full consent was given) and yet, on the other, failing to facilitate the moral development of the individual by diminishing the external pressure of authority.

We are only too aware of this paradox psychologically and there is really no further excuse now for perpetrating it. In particular, Western civilization must take serious note of the dangers of retarding autonomous moral decision in so far as such limitation is individually or collectively responsible for blind obedience which led to the Nazi crimes or the atrocities perpetrated in war. The ability to say No to authority on moral grounds is an essential component of mature behaviour which education must fortify fully in a world that has the means of massive human destruction through military aggression, and economic or political exploitation.

III Learning theory

As I have suggested, the word 'conscience' and the Freudian term 'super-ego', have the attraction of simplicity in that both describe a single, internal force or psychological mechanism that acts as an agent for distinguishing between right and wrong as assessed by the individual. This ability to evaluate from within, rather than respond simply to external requirements, appears about the age of four to six years and it means that the values of authority are taken in, are internalized, and become the standards of the child, so that they influence activity even in the absence of the external source of authority. But from this age onwards the child comes increasingly under the influence of other children, its peers, so that standards and values not only have two external sources of authority, namely parents *and* teachers, but adults are now in competition with peers and the influence of society in the form of classmates and friends. Charismatic figures become the other major source of moral values. Thus every adolescent and adult has the internalized value system of parents and other figures of authority; those of peers and society and of selected individuals, all of which contribute to the single described agency of authority. This much is clear from dynamic and Piagetian psychology, yet neither of these psychologies aims at describing the way in which human behaviour is actually acquired, maintained or changed.

For this, recourse is needed to a third major psychological theory, learning theory, which is associated with names like Pavlov (USSR), Hull,[22] Skinner[23] (USA), Eysenck[24] (UK). Everyone is familiar with Pavlov's classical experiments with his dogs. By studying a simple physiological activity like salivation he showed that new experiences can be learned. It is an ordinary observation both in animals and human beings that, in the presence of hunger, salivation occurs to a greater extent when the promise of food is at hand. In what has now become standard terminology the food is the *stimulus* and the salivation is the *response*. Thus there is formed (according to learning theory) a S–R link or bond. There are of course thousands of situations in which S–R bonds exist in life.

To the young baby, the face of its mother is the stimulus to comfort or reassurance of food or being picked up. In this way learning associations are developed throughout our life on the basis of reward, gratification or, more technically, reduction of drive. Hunger, thirst, sex and sleep are some of the obvious basic drives which demand satisfaction and the organism learns the most effective ways of accomplishing this. This learning theory, or behaviourism, is not concerned with feelings, emotions or intellectual processes. It is the least complicated of the three theories in that it simply describes what happens in practice. Animals and human beings have basic drives and many other more complex needs which are met through linking the need with an action that satisfies it. Such human activity occurs without the intervention of conscious, deliberate, willed thinking. We learn a series of responses which become part of our reflex, conditioned, automatic repertoire of behaviour. How is this accomplished?

For the most simple explanation we can return to Pavlov's experiments. Instead of the saliva flowing into the dog's mouth, it flowed into a tube and then into a measuring jug, thus measuring the salivation. This salivation increased when food was presented to the hungry dog. Gradually, in the presence of hunger, other preceding stimuli — such as the clatter of the food dishes or the sounds of those offering the food — could all produce increased salivation. The dog associated the preceding activity with the reward of the coming food and learned a *new* association. The clatter of plates or the noise of feet was clearly linked with the arrival of food. Pavlov showed that other signals such as a musical note could be learned by association, producing salivation and in turn were sufficient for salivation without the arrival of food. Thus a conditioned new response was developed. Furthermore, this conditioned response can be extended (generalised) in the sense that, provided the dog keeps on receiving its reward, i.e. the conditioned stimulus is rewarded with food, further response can be extended so that the dog is capable of responding to different musical notes. Conditioned learning can only be maintained if it is rewarded; if not, the response is extinguished.

So far the learning that has been described is that usually called classical conditioning, which refers to an inherited pattern of response, such as salivating, drinking to quench thirst, scratching to reduce irritation, and so on. But much behaviour has no such instinctual pattern of response. Humanity knew nothing about driving complex machines such as cars, planes, and so on; it had to acquire a new set of responses. Operant conditioning is the other form of learning. Here we are faced with a situation in which the organism has no in-built behaviour characteristics and the way we cope with a new situation is by trial and error or, more correctly, trial and success. Much of this type of operant conditioning has been carried out in laboratories on animals. In such experiments rats are placed in experimental boxes with a handle which, when pressed, provides a pellet of food or with an escape door when the surface on which the animal is standing is rendered painful by a mild electric shock.

Operant conditioning has extended the scope of conditioned learning because the animal can be carefully observed for various schedules of reward (reinforcement) or progressive elimination (extinction) of a particular pattern of behaviour. Now extinction can take place either by not rewarding or by *actually punishing*. The common fear of punishment (called aversive stimulus in the laboratory) can be — as already stated — an electric shock but aversive stimuli are infinitely wider in life outside laboratories. But one experience which is shared in laboratories and outside them, in animals or human beings, is the presence of pain, fear or anxiety as an aversive stimulus and much aversive conditioning depends on the mobilization of these physiological and and psychological responses.

At this point learning theory meets the expectation of the average citizen who associates all behaviour with rewards if it is judged to be right or good and punishment if it is judged to be wrong or bad and, furthermore, believes that all behaviour should be shaped and controlled by these two basic principles. Such simplicity seems to make any alternative suggestions superfluous or ridiculous. Furthermore, as far as children are concerned, the principal and basic need is to learn to distinguish between right and wrong, good and bad, a task which parents, teachers and authority have to discharge with appropriate punishment if necessary. The idea that punishment, which means aversive conditioning, should ever be questioned inspires the most powerful emotion amongst otherwise sober and highly sophisticated people. The hostile response is very natural, since all of us have been and are continuously conditioned by pain, anxiety and fear to shape our behaviour and the earliest figures who conditioned were parents, teachers and authority. The combination of authority and aversive conditioning is deeply ingrained in all human beings so that, when this combination of experience is questioned, either in terms of the significance of obedience or the need for punishment to shape behaviour, the overwhelming majority of human beings frequently find themselves at a loss as to alternatives.

This book is concerned to look more closely at both these characteristics whose very simplicity has mesmerized humanity for so long but, as far as learning theory is concerned, it certainly provides the scientific basis for examining the efficacy of aversive contingencies which is the sophisticated term for punishment used by Skinner in his controversial book *Beyond Freedom and Dignity*.[25] It is worth remarking here that such an eminent exponent of learning theory does not think highly of punishment as an efficient way of shaping human behaviour.

Be that as it may, we can now turn to consider human growth on the basis of learning theory. For this we turn to the work of R. Sears. Sears is an American worker who has tried to combine psychoanalytic insights with learning theory.

45

For him the key experience of the child is its dependency on parental figures, but principally on mother, for meeting its needs. It is she who supplies food and therefore the source of closeness, touch, warmth which become powerful signals of comfort, security and love. A child is in fact utterly dependent on mother for food, warmth, support, reassurance, security, with which is established a whole sequence of learning responses which are provided by mother. No one doubts that these habits learned in the presence of our mother which teach us how to please and placate and therefore elicit responses of love, form the basis, the infrastructure, of all future behaviour in circumstances when we want similar responses.

But as already noted from Erikson's work, indeed from common observation, the dependency needs are opposed by those for autonomy which occur very early on, indeed as far back as the second year of life. Here is then a classical and recurrent human drama. We require approval, affection, reward, love from another person, which means pleasing them, doing things their way and yet we wish to do things our way to retain our autonomy, not to become simple extensions of the other person. This battle of pleasing, placating and yet retaining our sense of autonomy begins in early childhood and the young child experiences the tension between pleasing and displeasing mother, the source and maintenance of life.

A good deal of the difficulties which adults have in asserting themselves, in detaching themselves from sources of authority which are at the same time providers of security, support, comfort, approval, in general of love, can be traced to the frustration experienced in these earliest years. Here is the learning ground of the tension between pleasing mother and therefore being rewarded by her, or displeasing her by asserting our independence and therefore attracting two sources of punishment, active punishment, physically or verbally, or the withdrawal of love.

In his early work Sears stressed the importance of this conflict in terms of frustration and aggression. Conflict between the desires of the child and that of mother produces frustration and aggression. The child screams, bangs, throws things, kicks to get his way. All these are means of releasing aggression and hence care must be paid to a vital point to which learning theory has drawn attention. The punishment of aggressive behaviour often occurs *after* the actual behaviour, after therefore the child has gained the satisfaction of releasing frustration and tension. The result therefore of the aversive effect competes with the satisfaction obtained by releasing aggression. Severe punishment, therefore, far from simply acting as a powerful inhibitor of 'bad' behaviour, fosters a vicious circle. The child resents the punishment and continues to need something which the parent will not provide, namely attention, the lack of which builds up to further outbursts of aggressive behaviour which releases the tension and this release is 'rewarded' by further punishment. This may of course become simply a negative attention seeking procedure. If the child doesn't get attention any other way, he will get it by bad behaviour which is rewarded in two ways; by release of tension and by getting some attention through punishment. Of course this is not the attention he really wants which is understanding, affection, care, love, but it is better than nothing.

Every worker in child guidance clinics, magistrate's courts and schools for maladjusted children knows that punishment, and particularly physical punishment, is no answer for children who appear to be stubbornly defiant, rebellious, disobedient, rude, in general difficult, and here more than anywhere else the authoritarian policy, which has no answer other than punishment, fails because behind the very 'bad' child is frequently the despairing, lost, confused youth who knows no other way of getting close to the source of love.

One aspect of adult masochism, the active desire for seeking pain as a means of stimulation, usually sexual in nature but taking other forms too, can be traced in some individuals to this form of negative attention seeking of childhood which was rewarded by pain and punishment. But even more common is the observation of many parents that a child is seeking a slap or a temporary sending out of the room, because this is the only way that the escalating frustration can be released. The expedient resort to either can be easily understood but expediency can become a dangerous learning response for the child if it becomes the predominant mode of seeking attention.

Physical punishment is most unsatisfactory and particularly dangerous because it may encourage masochistic traits later in life although masochism is rare, at least in its extreme form. Far more commonly physical punishment is potentially damaging because it arouses aggression in the recipient and it acts as a model to be copied so that the future parent has no better instrument for shaping behaviour.

The previous remarks might suggest that punishment is not an effective means of influencing behaviour. There was a phase of thinking in the thirties, forties and fifties when this view was held by some educators. Current research does not give support to this view. Punishment does alter behaviour[26] but the matter is not as simple as that. The evidence suggests that negative reinforcement of a specific response has a far more beneficial effect than the negative reinforcement of a situation. Sears expresses this another way when he says that punishing specific acts is more effective than an attitude of parental punitiveness.[27]

Not only is punitiveness as an attitude ineffective but a good deal of research suggests that the quality of the relationship between the agent who inflicts punishment and the recipient is a key element. Punishment is far more effective, as would be expected, when the agent is held in high esteem by the punished subject. Furthermore, in an impersonal situation the noxious, aversive factor (that is, the pain, fear or anxiety caused) is the major determinant, whereas even a mild threat becomes effective when the loss is that of the approval of a highly esteemed person. Finally, when punishment is increased it is effective when the relationship with the punisher matters but it is likely to generate further resistance if the source is unappreciated.[28]

All this suggests that the effect of punishment on children is far more than the production of an aversive reaction. This aversive stimulus is originating from parents who are a vital source of love to the child and the potential threat of withdrawal of love is in many ways just as, if not more, important than the physical distress of the punishment. The consequences of this rather common-sense observation has wider social repercussions for adults. When punishment is considered as a deterrent in the absence of a feeling of appropriate guilt by the person, or esteem for the agent who is imposing it, then in all likelihood it will be unproductive. Even worse, if its severity is interpreted as unfair or excessive, then it can easily become counter-productive and foster the spirit of revenge.

From what has been written in this section it can be seen that, as far as learning theory is concerned, conscience is the result of the accumulation of the appropriate learned conditioned responses. Furthermore Eysenck, who has put forward the theory that the human personality can be clearly divided into extraverts and introverts on the basis of their conditioned responses amongst other features, believes that since extraverts condition poorly they would be expected to have a greater preponderance, in all populations which are labelled and associated in some way with crime. He produces evidence to support this view.[29]

Thus there are men and women who are not only liable to be conditioned far less effectively to appropriate 'good' behaviour but for whom punishment as a conditioned deterrent effect is not so effective either.

Psychiatrists tend to see such patients in the course of their work, the extreme form of whom are called psychopaths, a not very clearly defined term, which usually implies behaviour characterized by limited capacity to cope with frustration, excessive and exaggerated response to it, marked aggressive and anti-social behaviour with little likelihood of responding to treatment. In addition to this pattern, psychopaths show impulsiveness, little concern for others, fragile attachments and sexual promiscuity. According to Eysenck, psychopaths fall clearly into the extraverted side of the dimension extraversion-introversion.

Not surprisingly psychiatrists find that the simple punitive reactions of society are not very convincing in the face of the wide variety of human personalities and in the knowledge that punitive handling simply does not affect certain personalities. Nor is this knowledge confined to psychiatry. Parents, teachers, indeed anyone in authority, know that whilst punishment can work, it frequently does not work so well and its failure cannot be simply ignored or dismissed as just 'badness' or 'stubbornness' or some other moral term which really explains nothing.

Learning theory suggests not only that it is important to teach and educate children by instilling the appropriate response and that punishment can be helpful, but that it has its limits. It is not very effective in the absence of an affectionate bond between child and parent or substitute authority unless it is so severe that it will prove counterproductive and this is unlikely to have any permanent effect. Finally training and punishment must take account of the personality of the child.

The other two theories previously presented also indicate that the age of the child, its level of psychological development and the emotional relationship between parents and children are all crucial factors in the development of a conscience.

From all this it can be seen that attempts to shape human behaviour which rely on the most elementary observations of blind obedience and fear of punishment, emanating from and applicable in the first few years of the child's life, are totally unsuitable for influencing behaviour later on when the growing person's and adult's autonomy, sense of equality, justice, altruism, aggressive make-up and loving response make a formidable array of deterrent factors in the response to, or threat of, punishment.

The average discussion of moral development rarely progresses beyond the simple and primitive concepts of early childhood to the later complexity of adult behaviour in any society where there is sufficient freedom to live at a level of sophistication extending beyond crude fear and pain.

NOTES

14   MAILER, H.W. (1969) *Three Theories of Child Development* (New York, London, Harper & Row)

15   FREUD, S. (1923) *The Ego and the Id* (London, Hogarth Press), pp. 35–6

16(a) ERIKSON, E.H. (1959) *Growth and Crisis of the Healthy Personality. Psychol Issues: Vol. 1*, pp. 50–100.

16(b) ERIKSON, E.H. (1968) *Identity, Youth and Crisis* (London, Faber & Faber)

17   CAFFEY, J. (1946) *American Journal of Roentgenology.* 56, 163.

18   Ref. 7; pp. 45–6

19   ACTON, H.B. (1969) *The Philosophy of Punishment* (London, Macmillan)

20   KOHLBERG, L. (1964) "The development of moral character and ideology", in *Review of Child Development Research,* Vol. 1 (New York)

21   KAY, W. (1972) *Moral Development* (London, Allen & Unwin)

22   HULL, C.L. (1943) *Principles of Behaviour* (New York, Appleton-Century-Croft)

23   SKINNER, B.F. (1938) *The Behaviour of Organisms* (New York, Appleton-Century-Croft)

24   EYSENCK, H.J. (1960) *The Structure of the Human Personality* (London, Methuen)

25   SKINNER, B.F. (1973) *Beyond Freedom and Dignity* (Harmondsworth, Penguin Books)

26   MARSHALL, H.H. (1965) "The effects of punishment on children: a review of the literature and a suggested hypothesis", *Journal of Genetic Psychology,* Vol. 106, pp. 23–33

27   SEARS, R.R., MACCOBY, E.E., & LEWIN, H. (1957) *Patterns of Child Bearing* (Evanston Ill. Row Peterson)

28   PARKER, R.D., & WALTERS, R.H., (1967) "Some factors influencing the efficacy of punishment training for inducing response inhibition" *Monograph of the Society for Research in Child Development,* Vol. 32, No. 1.

29   EYSENCK, H.J. (1970) *Crime and Personality* (London, Paladin)

Adolescence

For a superficial observer a description of the characteristics of equality, reciprocity, concern for others, equity, altruism ascribed to the later stages of development, that is to say the period of adolescence, from twelve years onwards to the early twenties, may bring a perplexed and cynical look. The adolescents whom parents, teachers, magistrates, law officers know are characterized primarily by disobedience, defiance, awkwardness, disregard for law and authority, insolence and general 'bloody-mindedness'. Once again there is just enough truth in this view to attract sufficient attention in any limited consideration of the subject. Equally, those who wish to praise young people for their kindness, generosity, courage, willingness to sacrifice themselves for others and can see nothing wrong in their exuberance tend to exaggerate the goodness of this phase of development, which is one of the most complex in the whole period of development.

In order to put these apparently opposing characteristics in perspective it is essential to understand, at least in outline, the principal features of adolescence. Adolescence must be placed in the context of the gradual separation between child and parent, a process which reaches its peak towards the end of the second decade of life. Much of the adolescent's turbulence will be found in this period of transition between childhood and adulthood when the young person is neither. No longer a child and yet often still treated as one both at home and at school; not yet an adult and yet treated by society, in the granting of certain privileges and responsibilities, as one, he is caught in an identity confusion, or what Erikson calls the phase of acquiring a sense of identity versus overcoming a sense of identity diffusion.

Parents find the changes of adolescence difficult to discriminate carefully and still have a tendency to treat their offspring as if they were younger children, an attitude epitomized by the title with which they refer to them. There is a fundamental difference between saying – 'This is my son/daughter' and 'my child'. They are surprised, upset, even horrified when their authority is flouted leading to endless arguments, quarrels and occasionally to physical conflict. Society has lowered the age for voting, marriage, owning and disposal of property, so that an eighteen-year old has all the privileges and obligations of an adult without the knowledge, experience or wisdom of action that he will have later on in life. But young people vote, marry, buy and drive cars, and who is to say that their actions are not wise? There are few adequate criteria to assess the outcome of such activity, with perhaps one exception. Statistics have shown repeatedly the dangers of early marriage as far as its breakdown is concerned. The earlier the age of marriage the greater is the statistical risk of divorce.[30] This outcome is not surprising, for the adolescent has to cope with four levels of maturity; physical, intellectual, emotional and social. Whereas they have reached the absolute peaks of physical and intellectual potential (though not most efficient utilization), they have yet to reach this in their emotional or social behaviour and, since marriage makes heavy demands on both these characteristics, the increased risks involved are understandable.

Adolescence is called by Erikson a 'psycho-social moratorium'. A moratorium is a period of delay granted to somebody who is not ready to meet an obligation or forced on somebody who should give himself time. By psycho-social moratorium then we mean a delay of adult commitments, and yet it is not only a delay. It is a period that is characterized by a selective permissiveness on the part of society and of provocative playfulness on the part of Youth, and yet it often leads to deep, if often transitory, commitment on the part of Youth, and ends in a more or less ceremonial confirmation of commitment on the part of society.

Currently many would say that society is too permissive and the playfulness too damaging and this opposition forms one of the central arguments between all those who feel authority should reassert itself and those who see the move towards greater independence as the correct one. What is missed by both sides is the need to accept that such a tension is an intrinsic part of the life of a community if it is going to facilitate the growth of its adolescents. It may wish to curb excesses or encourage more constructive expressions of aggressive playfulness; what it cannot do is to try to use authority to suppress the manifestations. The dream of every authoritarian parent, teacher and social legislator is the ability to 'stamp out' a particular form of disagreeable behaviour. As far as adolescence is concerned, the demonstration of independence, the defiance of authority and the expression of forcefulness are an essential triad of this period of growth. The direction can be guided but the components cannot be eliminated.

The social manifestations of aggression are obvious enough for everyone to pass judgment, which is usually condemnation, When it involves the wrecking of coaches in trains carrying football supporters, violence in the grounds, vandalism in the streets and mugging. All this evokes a sense of revulsion and horror and rightly so. Unfortunately the reaction is indiscriminate and misses the fact that the individuals who initiate such behaviour are almost always unrepresentative of the overwhelming majority of young people. What does happen, however, in a crowd is that many imitate, conform and comply, for these are the characteristic patterns of response for people of all ages brought up to follow a leader, in these situations a destructive leader. They conform and obey, they have been told to do that by parents and teachers but the leadership which they follow now is damaging. Parents and authority in general frequently complain that their children have got into bad company, which is pleaded in mitigation in courts and elsewhere. It is frequently the child or adolescent who is in the dock. The person who should be in the dock is the parent or society for failing to inculcate sufficient autonomy and independent judgment so that a destructive leader, be he someone who rips the seat of a train or behaves like Hitler, is not followed blindly.

It takes courage and judgment to stand up against others and this can only follow when the moral education that is given at home and at school encourages the growth of independence which is strong enough to withstand the collective pressures of groups. We have to go a long way to achieve this and, in the meantime, we respond to the adolescent behaviour by hoping for more suppressive control. This becomes inevitably one of the essential means of handling the situation when we are so limited in our alternatives. But one idea which rarely enters the discussion of those who come together to consider the appropriate response after another crisis is to consider the long term programme of moral education in our schools and homes.

It is these outward manifestations of social disorder which draw attention from the media and the censure of disapproval. In millions of homes the private and inward experience of the adolescent is that which matters to them, their parents and their immediate world. This inward world is characterized by a struggle which seeks to establish an independent identity of sufficient clarity and strength to negotiate the three major tasks of this age, namely to come to terms with sexuality, work and the departure from home.

Puberty is one of the earliest features of adolescence with the arrival of the secondary sexual characteristics of boys and girls and the invasion of the body by the appropriate sexual hormones. The adult sexual configuration with regular menstruation in girls, spontaneous nocturnal emissions in boys and the potential of sexual activity in both makes one of the clearest aspects of separation between children and their parents. The incest taboo is the barrier accepted by society as the visible sexual distance between the two. This imposes less strain on the parents who have each other for sexual outlet than on the adolescents, who have first to detach their bodies from the sense of *belonging* to their parents, particularly the mother.

The oneness which characterizes much of childhood has a marked physical component. The foetus lives for nine months in the womb of the mother, the young baby is handled as an extension of mother and this physical proximity is marked throughout the pre-school years and continues thereafter whenever physical attention is needed. The boy has a far more difficult journey of separation from the mother than the girl and perhaps one factor contributing to the more frequent sexual variations in men may be accounted for by this.

After puberty the adolescent has to complete the sense of possessing his body independently of his parents. One way is to experience sexual pleasure from self, hetero- or homosexual stimulation. This is not the place to argue the morality of such behaviour but to understand that the familiar criticism of all such behaviour on the basis of pleasure-seeking will just not do justice by itself to the complex motivation of the adolescent. This intrinsic source of physical experience, totally separate from parental influence, is one of the most powerful means of establishing a separate sexual identity. The knowledge acquired from the sensations of the body which followed physical experimentation are further extended by learning about its sexual functions and finally the social embellishment of covering it with suitable dress display which brings the adolescent into one of the commonest confrontations with parents. The arguments which on the surface appear to be a straightforward confrontation between 'No, you cannot wear that' and 'I jolly well can' are in fact far more subtle. The powerful but unsophisticated externalization of sexuality by the adolescent meets the ambivalence of the parents who want to relive their own youthful sexuality through their child but are burdened by the accumulation of adult inhibitions, fears and dread of what might happen if the dress emphasizes too much the body which the adolescent wants precisely to get to know. One way to get to know the body apart from its stimulation is through the attention it receives from others. Hence the battle between parents and adolescents, which is usually focussed on the dangers of permissiveness and the risks of sexual intercourse, is often really one aspect of the adolescent's essential need for physical separation from parents, particularly mother.

The emotional possession of one's body is a prerequisite for sexual functioning in relationships. The confident use of one's intellectual and physical skills is another prerequisite for independence. Nothing denotes the difference between childhood dependence and adult independence more clearly in social terms than financial independence.

But reaching the status of wage earner requires some clarity of thought about the type of training and work desired (provided there is enough of both to meet the needs of the unemployed). Every parent knows the confusion that can exist in adolescents about their study and work interests. Some adolescents are clear and precise about what they want to do; others are not. They do not want to do what the parents suggest unless the suggestion follows their own preconceived notions but, unless they know clearly what they wish to do, they may reject parental suggestions on the principle of rejecting everything the parents say. But the uncertainty can be most distressing since society requires that in theory they should now know, that they should be clear about their academic or working future. If they don't know, they are put in the awkward position of having to recognize their ignorance and, at the same time, avoid feeling that they are blindly following the leads given by their parents and teachers. In this quandary there may follow many hours of argumentative exchange, not because the dialogue is really evaluating the suggestions made by either side, but because the parent is at the receiving end of the frustration of their son or daughter who feel trapped in an impossible position regarding their independence which they cannot get hold of in the vital area of work.

Sometimes the fight is far more fundamental, that is to say when the adolescent is actively rejecting the attitude, values and standards of the work ideology of the parents, particularly the father. In the last fifty years the concentration of the conflict has been when the son or daughter of a working class family repudiates the parental standards and strives to move upwards in the social hierarchy or meritocracy. Recently a movement in the opposite direction has taken place when adolescents have repudiated the attitudes, values and standards of their middle-class parents. Study, business success, effort, conscientiousness, hard work and saving, the salient characteristics of the capitalist ethos, are turned down by young men and women who do not see much to approve in the capitalist society in which they live. It would take us too far from the subject of this book to consider this particular situation but the real issue is that society has now made it possible for the adolescent to repudiate parental standards with impunity. As in the case of the wife in marriage, neither economic nor social sanctions act as absolute prohibitions for adolescents who not only threaten to break from tradition but actually do so. In the past threats were part of an unequal struggle in which the parents more often than not held all the aces and, if one was missing, society with its authoritarian emphasis supplied the missing card to complete the quartet. Now the battle is far more equal. The rebellious adolescent will neither perish economically nor be ostracized by society. This growing balance between those in authority and those subject to it is one of the *salient features of contemporary society.*

The assumed possession of one's body and intellectual abilities leads ultimately to the severance of physical contact with parents; that is, leaving home. In those countries where military conscription exists, this period of transition occurs compulsorily at about the age of eighteen and the young man moves from one controlled environment to another. It is a useful transition.

In Britain and other countries that do not have conscription ·the exit from home is less clear cut and usually occurs by stages with long absences for holidays and other events. But the ability to live away from home is the final act of independence. Most adolescents achieve this without much difficulty. A few do not and very often the psychiatrist is involved in those instances which include young men and women too anxious and frightened to separate from the emotional dependence on parents.

The conflict in these homes is massive. Biological, physical, intellectual and social pressures are all driving the young person forwards, away from home, but anxiety and fear pull him backwards. There is, as might be imagined, a heightening of tension with marked aggravation of aggression which is directed towards the parents who are blamed for this situation. The various combinations of such family situations make up the material of psychiatric textbooks and we shall leave them there but, in the midst of the upheaval, the tension may become so marked that it is sometimes released by attempted suicide, acts of delinquency and self destruction through alcohol and drugs.

But the majority of adolescents leave home, start work or study and feel reasonably clear about their sexuality. Not all, of course, and the prevalence of less authoritarian standards means that a small proportion can escape from what they consider these intolerable demands by acts of defiance such as the refusal to work; joining temporary communes; or going for long journeys overseas and particularly in the direction of the East. These men and women are no longer persecuted but they are not exactly approved of either and they are variously called 'drop-outs', 'hippies', 'lay-abouts', and so forth. The terms vary from period to period and there is a tendency to use the most pejorative ones if the person also breaks the accepted codes of dress and hair style.

The customary debates about adolescents revolve round these topics which include their behaviour at home, at school and immediately after leaving both. Consideration of school will be given later but the adolescent who refuses to comply with the norms of society is often the target of the authoritarian moralist. They are described as lay-abouts, no good, who *should* be made to work, *made* responsible for their actions ultimately, of course, by coercive measures and punish-ment. Very little consideration is given to the reasons for such behaviour which may range from perfectly legitimate objections to the current values of society to the presence of marked personality distur-bance. Here often three erroneous attitudes are adopted. The first is not to differentiate the various groups. The second, from those who are orientated to the political left, is to interpret *all* such behaviour as legitimate political protest as if there was not room for debate and thirdly, to dismiss *all* these youngsters as in some way sick or disturbed.

In fact, what has happened is that a greater degree of permissiveness has allowed the emergence of behaviour which is no longer governed by fear. Thus adolescents rebel, wives leave their husbands, employees stand up to employers, and so on. Naturally all this is causing a great deal of anxiety in case anarchy and anomie win the day. Equally, instead of seeking to return to authoritarian enforcement of law and order as the only remedy, we have the opportunity to understand far more clearly the causes of such behaviour and the changing expectations of human beings at a critical period of transition in man's history, both of which are difficult to identify when conformity is bought at the price of submission due to fear.

But the average adolescent has no desire to cause more than the minimum of trouble. His energy is fully taken up coping with the transition from childhood to adulthood. The loss of security and dependence on parents means a welcome step forward towards further autonomy and additional anxiety, uncertainty, confusion, alone-ness and loneliness. The drive away from parents towards peers is now at its peak and with this psychological tendency other features are associated.

Piaget has shown that this is the phase when thinking can be carried out in the form of operations which are no longer concrete but formal which, as the words suggest, liberates the ability to consider thought and action completely without the presence of the concrete stimulus. Thinking can now assume abstract and universal qualities. At the same time, in the field of personal relationships, the trend towards autonomy is continued. Moral judgment is now not only based on equality but equity and a little more needs to be said about this word.

From about seven to about twelve, the child is steadily moving to reciprocal, equal relationships but the basis for the reciprocity is still governed by the presence of the rules available. They can now be changed by mutual agreement although they are still the basis of

57

governing behaviour. But there is clearly a stage beyond this which brings us to consider others as people with needs, feelings, motives, which go strictly beyond the legal requisites for the exchange.

The adolescent is now reaching the point of realising that reciprocity, which depends on equality and the law, is a minimum basis for what it is possible to give another human. Here other words like altruism are used and finally the most famous word of all, love. It is the ultimate of a morality based on personal values and we hardly need reminding that this is also the fulness of the Christian ethic.

This conclusion reached by Piaget has also been reached by others. Swainson[32] found a morality of love in her research and so did Peck and Havighurst[33] who considered that 'the rational-altruistic type describes the highest level of moral maturity'.

Thus adolescence presents one of the most contradictory pictures to the authoritarian personality. Here are rebels, opposing authority in all sorts of ways and yet simultaneously capable of spending hours attending to the needs of the elderly and deprived, showing fantastic loyalty and concern for their fellow peers, acting as leaders in many causes which are related to deprivation and poverty and giving generously of themselves and their natural goods for good causes.

This contradiction is in fact resolved when it is realized that this period of development represents the peak so far of the potential of independence and freedom from authority, combined with maximum awareness of the other person. This combination provides an ethic of behaviour which is truly capable of bearing the term of love.

There can be no real love[34] without a minimum level of separation from 'others', initially our parents, so that the consequent decision making can truly represent a genuine awareness of self and others and is not merely action which is a blind and compulsive extension of authority in our lives disguised as our own free availability of ourselves. The genuine awareness of self and others which is the fruit of this separation extends into the fullest possible possession of our physical, emotional, intellectual, social and spiritual dimensions and the sensitive recognition of these characteristics in others. The realization of this personal potential requires the fullest positive acceptance of self. I shall consider that in the next chapter.

NOTES

30   "Marital Breakdown" (1972) *Postgraduate Medical Journal*, 40, 563
31   ERIKSON, H.E. (1968) *Identity, Youth and Crisis* (London, Faber & Faber) p. 157.
32   SWAINSON, B.M. (1949) *The development of Moral Ideas in Children and Adolescents* (Unpub. D. Phil Thesis, Oxford).
33   PECK, R.H., & HAVIGHURST, R.J. (1960) *The Psychology of Character* (New York, Wiley)
34   DOMINIAN, J. (1975) *Cycles of Affirmation* (London, Darton, Longman & Todd) p. 2

Self~esteem

The work of Piaget was extended by Morris,[35] Peck and Havighurst, and others beyond the twelve-year-old stage up to later adolescence at sixteen, and the principles of reason, autonomy and altruism were generally confirmed. Thus there is now a considerable amount of research data which suggests that, by the time the young adult is ready to launch himself into adulthood, the criteria for moral judgments of behaviour are governed by the level of reasoning which can assess the facts of a situation, the descernment through feelings of the emotional needs of others and a sufficient internal freedom, not only to accept the existing rules but, if necessary, to modify them for the sake of what could generally be called love, even if that word is not always used clearly or precisely.

Clearly the ability to form this type of moral judgment about a situation depends on the level of intelligence and therefore the consequent grasp of its totality, awareness of others, particularly in terms of feelings and courage, motivation and absence of fear to respond fully.

One feature which does not receive extensive or detailed examination in this type of formulation of the mature moral judgment is the quality of experience of self. Piaget has used the term 'egocentrism' and has given it his own definition, but all psychological theory has commented on the child's intense self-interest, self-centredness, hedonism, awareness of self rather than the other in the early years of life. These psychological descriptions are concerned with the gradual detachment of the centre of awareness of the ego from parents and the incipient emergence of a self which has, in Freudian terms, given up the pleasure principle, the emphasis on gratification, and become aware of the reality principles in a reciprocal mutuality.

Dynamic psycho-analytical psychology, however, has concentrated most intensely on describing the feelings that we have about ourselves in the various stages of our development and ultimately in adulthood. The impetus for understanding these feelings came from psychopathology. The clinics of psychiatrists all over the world have a high percentage of men and women who consider themselves inadequate, unworthy, lacking in confidence and feel progressively bad, unwanted and unlovable. These feelings are frequently ascribed, particularly in adolescence, to some physical defect usually located in the face. Distortions of the nose, mouth, lips, teeth, ears are frequently given as the complaints responsible for the poor image of themselves. Sexual reasons also come high, girls being very conscious of the appearance of their breasts which are usually described as underdeveloped, and boys the size of their penises. Plastic surgery is sought and can, where there is a truly disfiguring situation, transform the outlook of such a person.[36]

But there are dangers. First of all, frequently there is no physical deformity to correct and, secondly, if no proper evaluation has taken place, surgery is followed by a worsening situation because the operation and the possible physical alteration were the last hope of a person who did not realize that his misery really did not emanate from his physical appearance but from his poor self-esteem. When the last possible excuse for his present state, namely his physical appearance, cannot give him the much sought-after relief of feeling good, his world breaks down into a state of severe misery and depression.

Most people do not have such severe problems of self-esteem but no one is free from this colouring of self. What is meant by self-esteem? Coppersmith gives this definition: 'By self-esteem we refer to the evaluation which the individual makes and customarily maintains with regard to himself: it expresses an attitude of approval or disapproval and indicates the extent to which the individual believes himself to be capable, significant, successful and worthy. In short, self-esteem is a personal judgment of worthiness that is expressed in the attitudes the individual holds towards himself. It is a subjective experience which the individual conveys to others by verbal reports and other overt expressive behaviour'.[37]

Clearly our self-esteem varies between one activity and another. People have different aptitudes and abilities. They can be effective in one activity and poor in another. Poverty of self-esteem becomes serious when it is a feeling judgment which is primarily incongruous with reality. In such situations, a person has a high level of competence objectively but assesses it otherwise intellectually, or recognizes the talent intellectually but devalues it in feeling: 'Yes I am good, but it is nothing, it really is of no significance.' Immediately after such personal devaluation he will pour out examples of what others can do – which is usually more and better than his own achievements.

But it is not so much in the assessment of functioning capacity, efficiency or competence that a poor self-esteem is damaging as in the global feelings, the enduring image such subjects have of themselves. It is their inability to feel worthy, good, of value, significant or lovable as people that has the most destructive impact.

Persistent devaluation stops such a person from aiming at an appropriate intellectual, emotional or social goal. This severe self-judgment means that he is constantly unable to feel that others enjoy his company, or could possibly appreciate him, since he is convinced of his own insignificance, lack of physical beauty, social charm or intellectual prowess. At the extreme end of this scale not only does the subject feel unworthy but positively bad, and this sense of personal rejection keeps him aloof from others and may lead ultimately to self-destruction. The most complete form of self-destruction is of course suicide, but there are other forms, such as alcoholism or drug addiction, which temporarily remove the intense feelings of badness or discomfort, allowing some rapprochement with others.

At the heart of promiscuity, too, lies the problem of total absence of self-esteem. Here are men and women who have such poor opinions of themselves that they cannot sustain any prolonged personal relationship, convinced as they are that they are emotionally incapable of receiving and giving the feelings needed to prolong the relationship beyond a fleeting period. This is due to a combination of constitutional and environmental factors which render such a person restless, deeply dissatisfied, craving for temporary stimulation and gratification, but unable to have any continuous and lasting relationships.

The negative consequences of such poor self-esteem are all-pervasive, and one of the three giants of psycho-analysis, Adler[38],[39] made feelings of inferiority the cornerstone of his theory. Neurosis for him was due substantially to these feelings, and many of the patterns adopted to overcome these feelings constitute the principal manifestations of neurotic difficulties. No one would disagree with this view today, although there would be extensive discussion about the factors that contribute to this poverty of self-esteem.

What does contribute to lack of self-esteem? As has been repeatedly pointed out, the constituents of the human personality reflect the genetic inheritance of the individual, and the subsequent environmental shaping of the person in the encounter between the child's potential and the parental response, aided and abetted by the influence of other authority figures such as teachers. As far as the make up of the individual is concerned, it can be said without any doubt that the vast majority of those who lack self-esteem tend to be anxious people, even though they themselves would not necessarily recognize this. A tendency towards an over-anxious response to stress can easily create an attitude of defensiveness to life. But there are of course anxious people who have high esteem and so this is not an absolute reason. It will be remembered that, according to Eysenck's theory of personality, extraverts do not condition as well as introverts and therefore do not register easily experiences of approval or disapproval. But frequently there is a contradiction between the outward appearances of extravert behaviour which gives the impression of a jolly, friendly, talkative, ebullient, hearty, eager to be involved person giving an air of confidence and certainty, who in fact, on closer acquaintance, is found to have an inner world of uncertainty, shallowness and lack of strength with poor self-esteem which does not match the outward appearance at all. This is of particular importance in marriage when either partner may be seeking unconsciously a reliable, secure partner and is deceived by the external joviality and bonhomie, because in fact the inner person lacks confidence and is full of doubts and uncertainty about his or her capacities. These and other constitutional factors certainly contribute to lack of self-esteem. But what is even more clear and certain is that the atmosphere within which the child grows up contributes to his sense of personal meaning. This is not surprising in the least when we consider how much we rely on our parents for our identity.

From what has been written already the outline of the parents' role is clear. Children need material care for survival, intellectual stimulation and a constant stream of affirmation in a process of growth which confirms their separateness and personal value at every stage. Few parents are negligent or deliberately cruel although cases of negligence and cruelty exist by the thousands. The overwhelming majority of parents provide the rudiments of material care although clearly this will vary from one environment to another. But neither poverty nor riches controls two things. Firstly the ability of a parent to make it consistently clear to the child that he is a person in his own right whose value is intrinsic to himself and is not dependent on being an extension of parental existence. Secondly, all parents can not only give their child the sense of his own independent meaning, but can confirm and affirm his automous achievements at every stage of his development.

These two points are highly relevant for the family, school, church or social structure which is primarily authoritarian in character, and in which other criteria have prevailed. First of all, dependence on parents has been a principal feature. Independence has had to be controlled, regulated, governed by the wisdom and sanctions of the system. This has meant that dependence has been encouraged and the emergence of a separate autonomous person discouraged or delayed. Secondly, goodness has been seen most clearly in terms of obedience, compliance and conformity. The growing person feels good when he complies, pleases, and placates. He feels bad when he does the opposite.

This pattern means that the child's good feelings really depend on parental opinion, attitudes and values rather than on the child's experience and achievements. When these are praised, they are praised because they please those in authority so the child gradually grows up with an outer layer of 'goodness' which is compliance and an inner layer of variable emptiness or badness which is the real self.

Psycho-analysis has penetrated this complex in some detail. The natural orientation of the child is towards autonomy and the acquisition of more and more talents. The really facilitating parents acknowledge and appreciate this constantly. The authoritarian parent is concerned with instilling 'goodness', 'obedience', 'good manners', and 'religion', based on fear, and is only concerned that the child should behave according to these criteria. Here is an impossible situation for the child. His inherent needs of approval, appreciation and gratification for his own achievements are ignored. In the early years of development parental behaviour is seen as absolute and is imitated, and if parents demand this type of behaviour, then clearly their conduct is the best while the child's wishes are bad. Gradually the child begins to feel that wanting anything for himself is bad and that goodness is only related to pleasing others. Later on in life such men and women, totally devoid of any sense of approval from others for their own achievements, fill the ranks of those who feel that they only exist to the extent that others approve of them and when that approval ceases or is in doubt, they feel totally empty.

In this type of authoritarian home, goodness is built on the principle of avoiding the forbidden, clearly prescribed by rules and regulations, violation of which warrants punishment designed to help the growth of goodness. Here are the circumstances in which goodness is based on the principle of avoidance of badness, rather than on affirmation and confirmation of personal value. *This great divide is surely one of the key elements of all education at home and school and the most basic issue to be resolved for any society whether it be one of Christianity or humanism.*

There is no doubt that up to now much of this concept of goodness, seen as an expression of avoiding that which is disapproved of by authority, has dominated much of secular and Christian life. Throughout the world people of all ages are now challenging this, and the outcome of this challenge will have the most profound social, moral and theological implications for life in the future.

In a previous study,[40] my own position was made unequivocally clear. There is no future for goodness if it is not based solidly on affirmation of human behaviour so that actions, feelings, words and thought are invested with their own intrinsic worth which by right belong to the child whose goodness does not depend on the whim of parents. As a psychiatrist I see too many people with little or no self-esteem going through their life as prisoners, depending on the goodwill and approval of others for their survival. They live by kind permission of others and that is no way to live.

Another characteristic of this type of authoritarian upbringing is the creation of what the Freudians call a powerful super-ego. The super-ego is the internalized attitude of parents. Every violation of authority's wishes activates a powerful emotion of fear, shame and guilt and this type of overscrupulous, extremely conscientious person can suffer havoc in his life because the slightest transgression, real or imaginary, causes an excessive panic reaction which is saturated with these feelings. Certainly a number of those who attended confession regularly in the past came from the ranks of such personalities. When the tendency to self-accusation was excessive and obsessive in nature, even priests came to realize that there was something wrong. But there were, and still may be, people whose confession has a great deal more to do with being a conditioned reflex for reducing anxiety associated with the sense of badness, than with using the sacrament as a real progress towards personal maturity and moral growth. Indeed, there *cannot* be such development unless the penitent can be encouraged to move towards greater self-autonomy and self-esteem. The future of this sacrament is intimately related to a deeper understanding and appreciation of the human personality and its intrinsic worth, a point which will be further considered.

Such a view of goodness runs contrary to views held for so long that any detailed research evidence in its favour, apart from the extensive clinical evidence of the dangers that lack of self-esteem inflicts on human beings, is worth recording. Two workers tested the relationship between dishonest behaviour and self-esteem by giving the participants a flattering or derogatory assessment of their personality from the results of a personality test. The results were deliberately falsified for the experimental situation. They found that low self-esteem increased the incidence of subsequent dishonest behaviour when compared with a group that had no such feedback.[41] Studies with delinquents not only show that they come frequently from homes where the children are unlikely to experience acceptance[42] but specific studies on their own self-concept suggest that it is less positive than in non-delinquents.[43] In the important field of altruism a number of studies suggest that altruism is positively related to self-esteem and its accompanying confidence.[44, 45, 46]

Finally, investigations in terms of friendship and courtship suggest that self-esteem plays an important part in the freedom of approach and the likelihood of maintaining relationships in which self-esteem is at the same level.[47] There is recurrent clinical evidence of difficulties arising in marriage when the low self-esteem of an individual causes him or her to marry someone who is of a lower social rank, and the marriage fails to work because of the resultant discrepancy of values and attitudes.

The evidence could be extended to show the unique place of self-esteem in the structure of behaviour and relationships. This chapter so far has shown possible antecedents, and will conclude with a reference to a very detailed study of the family structure of self-esteem,[37] showing that an antecedent is the presence of parents who show a high degree of acceptance, respect and clear firm rules. The presence of acceptance and respect is really no surprise but a further comment is needed on the functioning of firm but clearly delineated discipline.

It is frequently assumed in discussions and debates that those who favour a move towards autonomy, egalitarian relationships, critical evaluation of authority and the elimination of blind obedience, wish to eliminate all authority, particularly parental. Such an interpretation of motives does little justice to the authors of such views. Total permissiveness in upbringing is as damaging as authoritarianism. The reason why so much attention has been given to the latter is that it is by far the commonest pattern in our society.

Firm, clear, consistent parental authority is an essential component of growth. Children need a model from which they can learn and they need to be safeguarded against impulses which they cannot control. They cannot learn from parents who use authority as a substitute for example. This is the difference between authoritarian parents, who work on the principle 'Do as I say not as I do', and those for whom authority and discipline are expressions of their conviction in the value of the standards that they themselves live by and who give a variety of reasons for these standards, defending and discussing them and if necessary, changing them if they are inadequate. Above all, such a parent knows that there is a period for exercising absolute authority, and there is a period, which rapidly increases with the passage of time, for substituting for authority the appropriate encouragement of a child to reach as many decisions as possible on the basis of his own assessment of the situation.

Most important of all, children who are brought up in such an accepting, firm environment, where they feel cared for and respected, respond to sanctions because the source that applies them matters. The response no longer emanates from fear but arises because there is a bond of love.

Finally, it might be argued that this emphasis on self-esteem is an attack on humility. Perhaps no word is subject to more excessive and incorrect use than humility. Usually it is used in a context where it denotes disapproval of those considered to be self-congratulatory, those who exaggerate their own self-importance, inflate their potential or achievements, and make unwarranted claims. Such disapproval is perfectly justified.when this behaviour is compared with the reality of the situation, and it is found that truth is being violated. Unfortunately such an attitude frequently extends its basis of critique to disapprove of all feelings of approval, appreciation and congratulation of self.

A false view has emerged within the Church and without, that decries any and all behaviour which is self-laudatory. Such an attitude on the part of parents and teachers is of course utterly destructive of the development of children who, as has already been suggested, are brought up to feel and believe that goodness is reached by avoidance of badness and know very little of self-affirmation.

The wrong use of humility has also meant that the infinitely more difficult task of helping young people — and adults — to reach an authentic and accurate evaluation of themselves is inhibited by an approach which praises self-negation. Instinctively, young people and many others are revolting against such a view of life and they are of course perfectly correct.

The virtue of humility has no relationship to a pessimistic, negative, reductive outlook. As it has been argued at length elsewhere,[40] the true Christian approach incorporates two features. The first is the pre-Christian concept of a valid and accurate knowledge of self, the Socratic approach of knowing oneself, coupled with Christ's example of making oneself available to others on a basis of loving service. This availability is not based on emptiness and shallowness but on fulness. Christ emptied himself for others because he was the fulness of all being. He certainly had no problems about a false sense of humility. He knew who he was, where he was coming from and where he was going and his total availability to others was based on a personality that knew itself fully and neither exaggerated nor underestimated its intrinsic worth. Christians can do no better than imitate the Second Person of the Trinity by pursuing the development of their own fulness so as to be available as fully as possible to others.

Such availability is always related to the capacity to receive and give love. Children who grow up feeling that their legitimate need for attention is bad, continue to regard their needs in later life in the same way and find it very difficult to negotiate, receive or retain attention from others. Their inability to receive attention is camouflaged under the label of 'humility', but often their deprivation becomes the basis of envy and hostility towards others who are not similarly inhibited.

Furthermore, such 'humility' can often be a cover for an inner emptiness, and to the inability to receive is added a pronounced difficulty in giving to or loving others, and the combination of difficulties is rationalized under a variety of moralistic terms. True humility is not based on the encouragement of improverished self-esteem, but is linked with an honesty, the principle of reality in psychological terms, which seeks to rectify limitations as the basis for further personal growth, which in turn means greater availability, service and love to others.

NOTES

35   MORRIS, J.F. (1955) *A Study of Value Judgements in Adolescents* (Unpub. Ph. D Thesis, London)

36   OLLEY, P.C. (1974) *Brit. Med. Journal,* 3, 248

37   COPPERSMITH, S. (1967) *The Antecedents of Self-Esteem* (San Fransisco, Freeman)

38   ANSBACHER, H.J., & R.R. (Eds.) (1956) *The Individual Psychology of Alfred Adler* (New York, Basic Books)

39   ANSBACHER, H.L., & R.R. (Eds.) (1965) *Superiority and Social Interest* (London, Routledge & Kegan Paul)

40   DOMINIAN, J. (1975) *Cycles of Affirmation* (London, Darton, Longman & Todd)

41   ARONSON, E., METTEE, D.R. (1968) "Dishonest behaviour as a function of differential levels of induced self-esteem". *Journal of Personality and Social Psychology,* 9, 121

42   COWIE, J., COWIE, V., SLATER, E. (1968) *Delinquency in Girls* (London, Heinemann)

43   LIVELY, E., DINITZ, S., RECKLESS, W. (1962) "Self concept as a predictor of Juvenile Delinquency" *American Journal of Orthopsychiatry* (32,159)

44   LONDON, P., BOWER, R.K. (1968) *J. Social Psychology,* 76, 19-30

45   GORE, R.M., RUTTER, R.J.B. *J. Personality,* 31, 58-64

46   MURPHY, L.B. (1937) *Social Behaviour in Child Personality* (New York, Columbia Univ. Press)

47   MURSTEIN, B.I. (1971) *Theories of Attraction and Love* (New York, Springing Publishing Co.)

Marriage

The relevance of authority, obedience and self-esteem to marriage is very great, because they are intimately related to certain prevailing features of marriage today. These features are: firstly, the changing status of women; secondly, the changing pattern of marriage; and thirdly, the high rate of marital breakdown.

The changing status of women has been written about extensively from a variety of angles. The militant approach[48] to the development of women's emancipation has many champions, Sheila Rowbotham,[49] the far from militant Greek author,[50] Arianna Stanissopoulos, the Rapoports, who have documented some of the implications of dual-career families[51] and work for women;[52] and a brief chapter appeared in an earlier work of mine, *Christian Marriage.*[53]

There can be no doubt that the subordinate status of women which has lasted for thousands of years is giving way to an egalitarian relationship with men. It is extremely sad to reflect that this undoubtedly basic Christian concept has had next to no major support from the Christian Churches; most of the initiative has come from outside its ranks. There are, of course, exceptions, and individual Christian men and women have supported the movement for liberation but, as in almost every other aspect of sexual emancipation, the Christian community has been conspicuous for its disapproval, displayed in its initial lukewarm reception or passive resistance to change, offering a multitude of opportunities to those who want to attack its attitude. This is particularly sad because of the attitude of Christ himself, whose relationship to women showed he would have approved of much, if not all, of the main ideas of the emancipation movement. However, if Christianity has been slow to take emancipation under its wing, a combination of genuine respect for women, coupled with the principles of emancipation, should make a very powerful Christian platform in the future.

This, of course, has already had immediate repercussions in the context of marriage. Few contemporary women in the west to-day marry with the notion of obeying or submitting to their husband. This is not to deny that cultural and social class characteristics may still perpetuate a respectful attitude in some sections of the community, but it is no longer reinforced by the cultural norms propagated by the most powerful sources of attitudes, the public media of television, radio, films and press. In all these the principle of equality is being emphasized and the continuing move towards economic independence supports at a practical level the ideology of equality and justice. It is possible that economic reversal or strain may arrest or even reverse the progress but, short of large scale economic catastrophe, the trend is towards greater equality, which has profound implications for the marital relationship.

The most obvious consequences have been those that can be described and enacted in legal terms. The contractual terms of marriage have been gradually changing, extending more and more privileges to the wife in terms of her income, property, freedom of action, and providing far more generous financial terms should the marriage break down.[54] The changes in personal relationships are far too subtle to describe, not only because frequently there is a mixture of the traditional and the new existing side by side, but also because the changes are ultimately psychological in nature and defy the clarity of legal transactions.

Broadly speaking, however, one pattern can be seen and has frequently been described. This is a move from traditional roles to egalitarian relationships. In the former the husband and wife have certain traditional roles to fulfil. The husband is still considered primarily responsible for earning the main income, acting as the source of authority, protecting the family physically and materially and, until recently providing intellectual resources. Women on the other hand were expected to manage the home, have children and rear them, and act as the principal agents of affection and comfort.

It is perfectly true that, even in this traditional model, the personal characteristics of the spouses meant that the roles were modified, sometimes even reversed, but society and the Church expected spouses to conform outwardly to the traditional norms, whatever the reality may have been within the confines of the home.

The egalitarian relationship of to-day is founded on different beliefs, even if in practice much of the traditional role is preserved. Nevertheless practice is certainly changing and is carefully documented. However, it is not the task of this chapter to go any further with such a description, except in its implications for the husband-wife relationship.

When equality is presumed, and traditional roles are simply guides with practical but no social or ethical obligations, then the spouses have to base the activities within their relationship on a continuous series of renewed and renewable agreements about their mutual functions. On the one hand such a procedure gives infinitely greater freedom, flexibility and fulfilment when there is agreement, on the other it can and does lead to confusion, misunderstanding and stalemate which is resolved ultimately by the divorce court.

Like the adolescent, the wife cannot easily be made to obey and conform on the basis of fear, sanctioned by the community, and the implications of this are truly enormous. However, within marriage a great many personal wishes may have to be sacrificed for the benefit of the other members of the family. It is also true that fear may operate in individual circumstances. The recent interest in battered wives has brought into the open what every psychiatrist and social worker knows, that there is still much violence within the family. But such violence is contained within certain limits and there are today infinitely better opportunities of escaping from it.

Families gripped by violence and fear are a minority. The majority are able to structure their relationships on the fulfilment of mutual needs by making continuous adjustments on the basis of complementarity and equality. Such an approach means that the actual relationship is a far more intimate one. The difficulties arising out of openness, such as the loss of clearly delineated sex roles, have been compensated by emotional closeness of an unprecedented degree. Couples react nowadays far more spontaneously as they feel and not as they *ought* to feel and act.

Such spontaneity means that the marital relationship assumes much of the emotional closeness of the early years of childhood, and in many ways the modern egalitarian marriage relationship, which emphasizes the importance of feelings and instinctual fulfilment, resembles the uninhibited spontaneous experiences of childhood. There are of course marked intellectual, physical and social changes, but the greater the mutual freedom and openness of the couple, the greater is the expectation of emotional fulfilment.

One particular aspect of this emotional fulfilment, which is very different from that of childhood, is the challenge of how two separate, autonomous, adult people can meet, interact, fuse and yet not be absorbed or overwhelmed by each other. The whole essence of contemporary egalitarian marital relationships is this ability to relate on the basis of personal donation and fusion without the loss of personal identity. In fact, a great deal of the moment-to-moment squabbling, arguing, discussing between spouses is a constant searching for complementarity without loss of self-esteem. It is an interaction between social, intellectual and spiritual equals who are differentiated by physical and personal characteristics. Perhaps the pessimistic description

71

is the 'battle of the sexes', whereas the optimistic description is the 'creative interaction of the sexes'. And certainly, as parents, they have distinctive sexual functions to perform, both in the creation and education of new life.

The opposite of a creative interaction is a failure in the marital relationship. There are of course many reasons for this ultimate severance of the bond, but one pattern which stands out very clearly is intimately related to the subject of authority and obedience.

Research[55] and ordinary experience suggest that spouses are often attracted to each other because of marked differences in make-up. One feature that stands out is the dominance of one and non-dominance of the other. One partner appears to be extravert and the other introvert. In practice either spouse can be assertive, outgoing, or 'strong' but often in the marriages that run into difficulties it is the husband who is thus described. Frequently the story is of a marriage in which the wife is initially happy to be passive, and obedient. The husband's wishes and decisions govern the whole range of married life; the hours he works, where they live, the site of their holiday, their friends, the way money is spent and so on. For a while the wife is happy, or at least accepts the situation, even if married life is punctuated with occasional arguments. For wives brought up by traditional Christian ideas, there is, in addition, a fairly strong social and religious backing to preserve such an attitude.

This is clearly an unsatisfactory relationship because it creates strain. In the beginning habit, fear and confusion force the wife to accept a great deal that sounds and feels unsatisfactory because she does not have the confidence or skill to assert her own point of view, but gradually over a number of years her confidence grows, and her attitude of dependence and compliance changes to one of contradiction and challenge on both major subjects and details. If the husband does not accept her point of view, but insists on adopting an authoritarian stance, the result is an escalation of quarrels, arguments, and fights which may include physical violence, until the relationship can no longer stand the strain.

This delayed maturation of individuals who in their late adolescence are still shy, anxious, and passive, into vivacious, self-assured, active people is probably one of the most important contributions to marital breakdown in the first dozen years. It has also produced a sizeable proportion of those who have left religious life and the priesthood. Clearly this maturation is a complex psycho-social process of the personality and has to be recognized in its own right. What Christian marriage has to recognize is the presence of this change, and it must not compound the difficulties by encouraging any artificial dependence, particularly on the part of the wife, which will aggravate the inherent difficulties of the personality.

This is especially important at a time when divorce has become more acceptable than at any other time in the history of Christianity. The traditional response of Christians has been to describe divorce as an evil, and to hope that the moral indictment will prove sufficient to reverse the tide, but this attitude has met with complete failure and the referendum in Italy in 1974 showed that, even in the heart of Catholic Italy, divorce has come to stay.

Few people will deny the problems that divorce creates and the immense suffering associated with it:[55a] Christianity is perfectly correct in supporting the monogamous, life-long relationship. This was Christ's specific recommendation and it gives Christianity one of the clearest principles to advocate, but the likelihood of success is only going to increase if it is recognized that global admonitions will go on failing unless they are coupled with a clear recognition of man's changing consciousness of himself.

A woman's ability to assert her autonomy, to insist on a much higher standard of personal integrity in marriage, is now backed by social and economic support which makes it possible, although still difficult, to turn protest into effective action. It could be argued that this privilege is used lightly, and it could be argued from fundamental Christianity that it is always evil. As far as the former is concerned there is no doubt that the motivation arising from Christian principles will act as a brake, a deterrent to any hasty action; but as far as the latter is concerned, there have always been provisions for giving relief to an intolerable marital situation and even the Catholic Church, with its most strict criteria, has used and extended these over the centuries.[55b]

The only effective answer today is to combine an orientation which acknowledges the ideal of indissolubility with an education which prepares couples for changing expectations that do justice to the contemporary man-woman relationship.

NOTES
48   MILLETT, K. (1969) *Sexual Politics* (London, Hart-Davis)
49   ROWBOTHAM, Sheila (1972) *Women, Resistance and Revolution* (London, Allen Lane)
50   STASSINOPOULOS, A. (1974) *The Female Woman* (London, Fontana)
51   RAPOPORT, R., & R.N. (1971) *Dual Career Families* (Harmondsworth,Penguin Books)
52   FOGARTY, M., RAPOPORT, R., & RAPOPORT, R.N. (1971) *Sex, Career and Family* (London, Allen & Unwin)
53   DOMINIAN, J. (1967) *Christian Marriage* (London, Darton, Longman & Todd)
54   MATRIMONIAL PROCEEDINGS AND PROPERTY ACT (1970)
55   DOMINIAN, J. (1968) *Marital Breakdown* (Harmondsworth, Penguin Books)
55a Ref. 30, p. 517   55b THE CHURCH'S MATRIMONIAL JURISPRUDENCE (1975), Canon Law Society Trust.

Authority and society

So far my analysis of authority has taken place in the context of the relationship between a growing individual and his parents, which reaches its conclusion in adolescence and in the one-to-one relationship of marriage. In the course of such development the individual is also influenced by other figures of authority, such as teachers, and at the same time increasingly relates to peers and friends. All these relationships are conducted with a high degree of personal intimacy.

As far as the first decade of life is concerned this intimacy between children and adults fosters certain basic characteristics in the personality. On the one hand there is a positive experience of being cared for, supported, comforted, understood and reached; in short, loved. On the other there is fear, awe and the feeling of guilt when authority is challenged and transgressed. But there is a delicate balance between love and anger, acceptance and rejection, respect and criticism, fear and admiration, autonomy and conformity, emulation and individualism in the presence of any personal bond.

When the individual leaves this world of personal bonds he enters a society which replaces personal characteristics with impersonal social structures in which there is group activity with maximum requirements of effective interaction and minimum personal bonds.

When a person leaves the confines of family and school, he enters the world of work, clubs, societies, organization and, by nature of being a citizen, society itself with its massive requirements for cohesion and conformity, which are necessary if it is to function at all and not break down into anomie and anarchy.

It is at this level that authority has experienced some profound changes which need careful assessment. There is a constant stream of bitter, and at times anguished complaints from people in all walks of life that the rule of law and authority is being threatened, and the end of civilization is round the corner. There is plenty of evidence of social instability throughout the world to justify this anxiety; individual and organized crime, civil disobedience, air piracy, senseless destruction of property and wanton aggression. However, what is not appreciated is that major changes in human consciousness require that these acts of lawlessness be assessed, both in quality and quantity, against the magnitude of human variation. In my view, when this is done, when disorder is put into perspective against the profound alterations in man's changing consciousness of himself, then the evaluation assumes a different and less sinister character. Certainly the usual conclusion that is invariably reached in such discussions, namely that what is needed is a return to sterner discipline, obedience and conformity, falls on deaf ears because, however attractive the notion is, obedience to authority can only be effective in a free society, in the presence of consent to and acceptance of the credentials of such authority.

The credentials of authority are defined in social terms by its legitimacy, by its effectiveness in terms of power and control, by its ability to preserve order and justice, by its means of redress against injustice, and ultimately by its efficacy; in other words, is authority achieving the ends it sets out to fulfil? The authority of local, national and international laws, and business and professional organizations are judged by these criteria. But these social criteria have to be judged by the way the individual experiences authority and here there are additional psychological factors operating which are highly pertinent in the process of change we are witnessing at the present moment.

The child's first experience of authority acknowledges none of the social characteristics just described. Instead his earliest concern is whether he feels safe and comfortable and can experience a sense of trust such as Erikson describes. In the depths of all human beings' involvement with authority is a discernment of care; is it present or absent?

But this sense of care rapidly develops in the next few years into a phase of fear. The child fears the power of the parents. This power can be marked physical force, loss of approval, rejection, abandonment or total repudiation. Fear plays a most prominent part in the relationship between those under authority and those in authority in all aspects of life hereafter.

Now this balance between the two forces, child and adult, gradually changes from the omnipotence of the parents to an increasing equality, with the ultimate goal, through progressive stages, of *equality of personal worth in the presence of persistent but diminishing differences of physical, intellectual, emotional and social capacity*. This is a very different concept from the ideology of absolute equality, which can never exist, and which fuels much ideological discontent and perversion of the authentic progress of social justice.

The growth of a personal relationship between child and parents

75

depends on the presence of sufficient trust, care and affection on the part of parents to give the child a sense of its personal worth in the absence of equality of function or capacities. This is achieved by the gradual separation and autonomy of the growing person who becomes increasingly less dependent on fear, sanctions and the danger of being overwhelmed by figures of authority.

What happens within the confines of the family is happening increasingly within different societies throughout the world. Thus the omnipotence of colonial powers is giving way to the independence of separate nations who can control their own destiny within their own frontiers. The guarantee of freedom for individual countries is a major objective in the world to-day and clearly it is far from being achieved. Eastern Europe is dominated by the USSR, and there are several parts of the world in which territorial disputes remain unresolved because of the presence of armed forces. There are also economic forces which the super-powers wield to the disadvantage of smaller countries. Here however a new balance is emerging between underdeveloped countries with primary commodities and the developed world so that a greater sense of equality is being achieved.

Within certain societies, such as that of the United Kingdom, there are marked changes occurring between those in and those under authority. One of the most obvious changes is in the world of business and industry. The marked dependence of workers on their employers, backed by the fear of dismissal and unemployment, is rapidly changing in favour of much greater equality between the two forces. Unfortunately the tension built up over a couple of centuries remains and a world of 'we' and 'they' still brings bitterness, resentment and at times hate. The Marxist critique of the workers' alienation is not removed in a Communist society which denies so much of the freedom of the individual that commercial exploitation may diminish at the price of even greater loss of personal worth and significance. If personal freedom is not suppressed then the goal must remain that of equality of personal worth in the presence of marked personal differences, something incidentally which society tries to bridge through monetary adjustment, paying different rates for different skills. Clearly this is only a partial and very unsatisfactory solution, because money can never replace the need of any individual for personal appreciation, independently of their objective contribution. This is something which the parable of the workers in the vineyard, who were' hired at different times of the day but paid the same amount, illustrates beautifully. The love of people is a greater force than either reason or simple principles of justice. Whereas Christ clearly sets out the appropriate principles they have to be worked out slowly in the context of different social conditions.

It is nevertheless clear that money can never be the ultimate means of offering and receiving personal recognition and one of the most urgent tasks that faces management and workers today is working out totally new criteria for effecting the ideal of equality of personal worth in the presence of complementary but differentiating personal capacities. Personal relationships are an all-important aim.

What has happened in industry is happening in every layer of society. Within individual companies the hierarchical structure is being replaced by changes in which authority is gradually losing its sense of absoluteness and becoming increasingly accountable for its actions to society as a whole and to those over whom it exercises authority.

These changes are seen particularly in the professional world of medicine, law, and in the life of the Church, where authority takes the form of consultants in hospital practice, doctors in general practice, judges, bishops, and priests. These people are no longer feared or considered omnipotent, but are assessed far more critically on the basis of their personal merit. This diminution of automatic respect for authority is a particular source of distress to authoritarian figures. Eminent people from all these professions pontificate about this loss of respect towards authority as if it is the greatest tragedy that can happen in society. Very often they have little conscious awareness that it is their own emotional immaturity which demands figures of authority that provide a sense of security as the source of ultimate wisdom, power and protection in order to safeguard them and the rest of society. What they are describing is not the loss of authority of such figures but their own inner anxiety which needs such figures in society to give them the continuous equivalent of parental protection. Incidentally it is these very critics who often have double standards of eulogizing the virtues of authority and yet exhibiting the worst authoritarianism in their treatment of all those below them. Nothing exhibits more clearly the psychological basis of anxiety of such histrionic complaints than the subservience shown towards authority by such people and their callous and indifferent behaviour towards their subordinates, or the disdain and contempt with which they treat anyone they consider their inferior. The hypocrisy which such a situation can create in society is gradually disappearing as the inauthentic ground or basis of authority is increasingly challenged.

Another complaint of authoritarian figures is that the diminution of the hierarchical structure brings a poverty of equalization, in which there are no distinguished figures left to be emulated. This is of course a nonsensical criticism because the distribution of talent in any society will always ensure that excellence is not extinguished and therefore there will always be men and women of talent who remain a source of inspiration for others. But ultimately, what society is seeking is that the model of authority should be one of integrity, wholeness, holiness, wisdom and love and not based on the power of money, coercion, violence and subjugation of others.

Part of the difficulty is that most societies are in various stages of transition from authoritarian patterns towards those of greater equality and mutual worth and the feature that stands out in practice is the conflict between groups, classes and organizations giving prominence to philosophies of conflict in society as an essential characteristic of progress or of conflict, resolution of conflict and then further conflict. One can see similar patterns in individual relationships where there is a continuous see-saw exchange in which the self-esteem of one person is achieved by the temporary diminution of the other and *vice-versa.*

Conflict as a permanent feature of society's development is a pessimistic and nihilistic philosophy based on the absence of mutual care and recognition; and that is one of the great dangers of urbanized society in which impersonality and therefore the absence of personal bonds is at its highest. In such a situation conflict will appear an easier alternative to the establishment of meaningful personal bonds. In pre-industrial societies meaningful bonds existed by virtue of the fact that the family and the means of production and consumption were very closely related to each other. With the gradual separation of all these constituent factors, society has achieved a major degree of impersonality which up to recently was camouflaged by the presence of authoritarian systems which, operating through fear, awe and economic dependence, retained a measure of cohesiveness. *The combination of industrialization and the gradual diminution of authoritarian systems is destroying cohesiveness and many of the disturbing symptoms in our society today are the fruits of the culmination of these two processes.*

The answer, however, is not to turn to the past. Humanity's social and psychological evolution cannot be dismissed; instead we have to look forward and construct new value systems based on principles of freedom, mutual worth and equality.

These are fine words, some will say, but irrelevant when the very fabric of law is undermined. This criticism is totally unjustified. My description so far has confined itself to the gradual but inevitably changing framework of relationships between those wielding authority and those submitting to it. There is, however, another aspect of authority, which is the citizen's responsibility to respect and uphold those laws which exist for the well-being of the whole society. Laws safeguarding the security of the individual and of others inevitably multiply in a complex society like ours. Respect for property, the safety of others, their freedom, their integrity, obeying the laws, regulations for health and so on bring in entirely different issues. Here respect for law is necessary for the functioning of society and in fact the overwhelming majority of citizens obey all these laws most of the time. There will always be a small minority who will not conform or comply. Such men and women exist in every society of whatever political persuasion.

It has been argued that because authority is being challenged – in my view legitimately – in terms of personal relationships, therefore anarchy in the wider sense is bound to spread and therefore society is at risk of breaking down. But here we have a basic and fundamental confusion. The evolution of relationships in society between opposing forces locked in authoritarian structures is one reality, acceptance of rules and regulations which safeguard the interest of society as a whole is another. These two realities are certainly confused and at the extreme end of this confusion will be found anarchist ideologies which claim that their philosophy is the only answer to society's problem and extreme left views that dream of such equality that sexual, intellectual and psychological differences will make no difference to social structures and relationships. Although these extreme views and opposition to them dominate much of the discussion of hope and fear for the future, there is left a substantial and important area of change in which authoritarian structures are being slowly changed by the realization of increasing individual status, dignity and significance.

This is a progress to be unequivocally welcomed whatever the short-term upheavals the change carries with it. It is important not only for the ultimate realization of greater justice, equality and freedom in society but as an effective counterpart to the bureaucracy of modern States. The industrialization, urbanization and complexity of modern western States have produced a degree of bureaucracy which, coupled with the impersonality of society, creates dangerous conditions in which laws have to be carefully evaluated by those who are asked to obey them. Ultimately cruelties like those of Nazi Germany, Stalinist Russia and other parts of the world can be eradicated only if the individual has enough authority in himself to challenge a state authority which contravenes basic morality.

The way in which legitimate authority is challenged is at the heart of much contemporary moral debate. The purpose of this chapter is not to discuss this matter further but to point out that an educational programme which aims to give a growing person the maximum sense of personal worth with the least intimidation by authority, offers the best background for evaluating all subsequent behaviour of authority, and challenging it whenever necessary, without the challenge becoming an extreme form of ideology such as anarchy or an egalitarian utopia. Normally the challenge will occur in small everyday events where authority has to be challenged because the combination of anonymity, impersonality and complexity makes it a recipe for inhumanity.

So far this chapter has dealt with the individual in big work organizations or as a citizen in society. Between the world of personal relationships in the family, among friends and in the wider circle of work and society as a whole, there are a host of intermediate situations. Men and women belong to sports clubs and other societies. They may participate in a temporary or *ad hoc* committee, and find themselves in several situations where neither the anonymity of a large organization nor the intimacy of the family is the only alternative.

These intermediate situations have characteristics of their own. Clubs, and indeed even small working units, have their own rules and regulations which must be obeyed if the objects of the society or organization are to succeed. But in these situations the impersonality of the occasion is markedly reduced. The approval and esteem of colleagues in professional bodies, and of fellow members of a club, monitor behaviour less effectively than the loss of love in personal relationships; but they do so more powerfully than impersonal rules or the absence of any such personal constraints in large organizations.

The breakdown of the unity between home, production and consumption which came with the industrial revolution has caused human relationships to be delineated for the most part between the intimate family and personal bonds, and the increasing loss of that significant emotional bonding as the individual moves into the wider circle of work and society as a whole. Nevertheless at all levels there has been a gradual decrease of relationships based on fear, awe, absolute respect or reverence in favour of a greater equality of personal worth. This change has taken place in the midst of conflict and strife wherever the impersonality and distance between two groups are greatest, and by mutual consent and constructive change when the desirability for change has been recognized as advantageous to all concerned. All societies are undergoing these changes with the accompanying repercussions which, in their extreme manifestations, appear to be violent and destructive. Yet in spite of the dangers, the benefits for human dignity are so great that the positive elements are worth close examination by those concerned about human values.

Authority and the Christian community

The Christian community is made up of all those members who through baptism share in the life of Jesus Christ. It has a special concern for human values. Within the visible Church, the body of Christ, its members should reflect most accurately the image of God in man and the kingdom of heaven should be most readily discernible. In the realm of authority the Christian community as a whole has failed to read the signs of the times accurately and its leaders, covering the whole range of denominations from fundamental evangelical Protestantism to Roman Catholicism, have made serious errors.

The reasons for this failure are threefold. The first has been to associate the kingdom of God with an authoritarian system, dependent on the use of authority as a source of power, generating feelings of fear and guilt in its adherents which are foreign to the message of the Christian Gospel, where authority is seen primarily as service[56] and where the essential message of love is incompatible with fear, a point beautifully and succinctly made by John.

> God is love
> and anyone who lives in love lives in God,
> and God lives in him.
> Love will come to its perfection in us
> when we can face the day of Judgment without fear;
> because even in this world
> we have become as he is.
> In love there can be no fear,
> but fear is driven out by perfect love;
> because to fear is to expect punishment
> and anyone who is afraid is still imperfect in love.
>
> *(1 John 4: 16–18)*

The second is the failure to discriminate between supporting law and order in the community, something that the basic conservative nature of recent Christianity has found easy to do, and the evolution of human relationships from positions which belong to early childhood

81

where inequality, fear and dependency predominate, to the more mature later stages in which maturity is seeking equality of personal worth in the presence of differentiating capacities and characteristics. Once again Christian leadership has failed to foster the kingdom of God where such mature relationships of equality reflect the spiritual equality to which Paul refers and which naturally belong to that kingdom: 'Before faith came, we were allowed no freedom by the Law; we were being looked after till faith was revealed. The law was to be our guardian until the Christ came and we could be justified by faith. Now that time has come we are no longer under that guardian, and you are, all of you, sons of God through faith in Christ, and there are no more distinctions between Jew and Greek, slave and free, male and female, but all of you are one in Christ Jesus' *(Gal. 3; 23–28)*.

The Christian community has to show the world the meaning of this kingdom which Christ has initiated. Instead of showing that our faith in Christ mobilizes a quality of love which establishes an absolute worth of the individual independent of race, status or sex, some Christian leaders have dared to use the scriptures as an argument for perpetuating humiliating inequalities of colour, race, sex and hierarchical, authoritarian structures, which have denied the elementary dignity and rights of individuals. There are very many individual and collective exceptions to these criticisms, but it is a pathetic commentary on Christianity as a whole that it cannot claim to be the unequivocal champion of any of the movements throughout the world that have fought for this equality of worth of women, and of coloured people, and against discrimination against minorities.

The third, and in some ways the most serious, failure of all is that the Christian community has fostered ideals which have encouraged the characteristics of early childhood emotional immaturity, and have perpetuated that immaturity in its various structures, particularly the priesthood.

This emotional immaturity has been partially covered by an excess of emphasis on intellectual skills and the apparent ease with which human problems were resolved, either by fundamental biblical theology or intellectual expertise at the extreme end of the Protestant-Catholic polarity, left a real vacuum in the lives of ordinary people which was obscured for a long time by the presence of authoritarian cohesion. When authoritarian structures were challenged in all denominations in turn, the absence of a real nurturing on sound principles of the kingdom has exposed Christianity to an unprecedented vacuum, and the challenge of fundamental rethinking which is going on at present and will have to continue for a long time before important breakthroughs occur.

In some ways the worst offence that any Christian, whether a bishop or an ordinary man or woman, can commit, is to support his own need for emotional security by expanding the kingdom of God in authoritarian terms. A world which is slowly grasping the meaning of maturity, intuitively, and through the psychological sciences, will not be misled by such exhortations, whatever the source; for maturity is incompatible with insecurity and inadequacy. But the yearning for God and the spiritual does not cease, hence the proliferation of fringe spiritual movements all claiming to answer the contemporary spiritual hunger. This hunger makes it essential for mainstream Christianity urgently to seek answers to contemporary problems. Among them is the right response to the challenge of authority.

The Christian community needs to show by the life of its members that it really understands the issues raised by the authority problem, and that it is beginning to give convincing answers, in theory and in practice. To show those answers in its people's lives it has to return to its source: the life of Jesus Christ.

The positive contribution of the Christian Community

First, Christians must clearly distinguish between supporting law and order in the community in which they live and the changes in personal relationships within that community that aim to foster the equality of personal worth in the presence of differentiating characteristics.

Now the implementation of law and order for the effective functioning of society, that is to say the protection of interests of all citizens against lawlessness, injustice, discrimination and the denial of basic rights of freedom, is something that Christians in common with all other citizens will wish to support. But in most societies there is a multiplication of bureaucratic rule which requires eternal vigilance to ensure that the support of legitimate authority does not encourage evil practices. Here mature evaluation of the actions of legitimate authority, not blind obedience to authority, is what Christianity must foster. Blind obedience is simply a perpetuation of early childhood life in which parents were perceived as almost invariably wise, right, omnipotent and all-powerful, deserving absolute and unquestioning conformity. Such obedience is immature servility and to foster it in contemporary societies with their considerable elements of impersonality and the absence of personal bonds is to risk a level of inhumanity which is inconsistent with the law of love, a primary consideration of the kingdom of God.

Christians must support the rule of law and legitimate authority but, at the same time, they must encourage educational principles which will arm the citizens with the means of ensuring that authority acts as a source of service to the community and not as a source of irresponsible power which moves from service to coercion, from care to subjugation, from encouragement of maturity to that of immaturity. One way of ensuring this is for the Christian community to offer an example in its own life.

As a Roman Catholic I belong to a world-wide Christian community which has excellent opportunities of fostering the principles enunciated throughout this book. Far from wishing to dismiss or destroy its hierarchical structure of pope, bishops, priests, nuns and laity, I am sure that its basic structure in terms of these offices is an appropriate one, provided that they are all seen, lived and offered as models of service and not copies of a secular power structure, operating on the principles of power, coercion, fear, guilt and massive impersonality. The Catholic community, in common with other denominations, has the responsibility — indeed the duty — to lead, to give an example of how authority should function by emphasizing the principles of service, maturity, availability, personal integrity and wholeness which are the marks of Christ's authority. Indeed, I see that an urgent task is for the Christian community to become a beacon of community relationship which emphasizes a progressive movement towards equality of worth, independently of personal characteristics. This has to be seen in the life of parishes, in religious communities, in the personal lives of Christians, in the theory and philosophy expounded in Christian writings, in the support given to organizations and movements which truly champion these principles and do not use the jargon of this language as a form of ideological propaganda whilst they contradict the principles in practice.

One of the essential features of such Christian life must be an attack on the impersonality of urbanized living. Nothing encourages contempt for law and order more than the distance separating those who promulgate the laws from those who have to obey them. The gradual separation between one human being and another, which industrial society has brought about by the structure of work, living conditions and breakdown of personal bonds, is an attack on the basic Christian concept of loving our neighbour. We cannot love the neighbour we do not know and with whom we have no personal links. In fact the heresy of our age is disposable relationships. By disposable relationships I mean the degree of alienation between employer and employee that makes market values the principle bond between the two, the degree of alienation between men and women that makes physical sex the most significant link between the two, the degree of alienation between one citizen and another that encourages an exploitation in which one human being becomes the stepping stone for the progress of the other.

The Christian community, concerned with authority as service, must begin to attack the heresy of disposable relationships, both in theory and practice. First of all it must ensure that relationships within itself assume a sufficient degree of intimacy to act as a deterrent for the impersonality to be found in society. I consider that the present parish structures are incompatible with such an aim and, if Christianity is serious about giving the world a lead, it must break down the pseudo-mutuality of its parish life which brings together hundreds of people on Sunday and leaves them miles apart for the rest of the week. The Christian liturgy must be celebrated in smaller units at all levels of streets, homes and other units so that those who proclaim the Lord as the source of love can translate this faith into the practice of loving their neighbour. They cannot do this until and unless they get to know him.

Here religious life must become one of the spearheads of genuine mutuality. The world knows the debt it owes to monastic life in the Middle Ages as the guardian of culture and civilised values. I believe that the religious life of nuns and monks must assume a fresh responsibility to show the world a degree of fraternal mutuality which will act as a living model. I have expounded these views in a series of articles.[58, 59] Here is a real opportunity to show how people of different backgrounds and talents can make an effective community of love if motivated by the principles of the kingdom of God. I look forward to the return of lay people flocking to these communities seen not as models of arid, authoritarian retreats from the world but as living fountains of community, mutual awareness, commitment, responsibility and relationship.

The next concern for the Christian community is the resolution of conflict. Here are philosophies which make conflict the inescapable basis of society's life. Christians must show that such philosophies are true heresies in the sense that the 'other' is only a suitable target for aggression, fight and defeat. On the contrary the 'other' is our neighbour and is not an object for aggression but for love. Love does not eliminate conflict nor even the expression of aggression as Christ showed in his own life but it demands principles of resolution which reflect justice and maturity. It is easy to resolve conflict by the exhibition of power in the presence of inequality between two sides. However, as equality of worth becomes more widespread, certain principles will need to be observed.

These principles require that the case of all concerned is heard and truly respected. Everyone has a right to be heard, if justice is to prevail. But the person needs not only to be heard but also to be understood. This is where so much conflict in society is perpetuated because the inner world of needs, aspirations, hopes is not appreciated or understood by the 'other'. Within the Christian community an attempt must be made to go beyond strict adherence to law. The Catholic Church is famous for its canon law and there is a great deal to be said in its favour in terms of clarity, comprehension and uniformity of application of principles, but the strict application of law can never do full justice to the inner world of a person whose motives and actions are infinitely more complex than laws can ever make allowances for. Thus the application of law, strictly and without favour or fear, is particularly effective where the contending parties have no bonds, no personal relationship.

Justice can only prevail by the strict application of legal principles. The Christian community must aim to penetrate beyond such impersonality and the return of canon law inside the Catholic Church, much favoured by those who basically cherish authoritarian principles, can also impede the progress towards a real Christian community. Ideally there has to be a balance between law and love but there can be little doubt that love must be at the centre of the Christian life and law at the periphery. If that is truly the case, then conflict becomes much less likely and the resolution of conflict a less difficult matter. Certainly law is the only means of resolving conflict in impersonal and anonymous relationships but the aim of the Christian community must be to reduce anonymity and impersonality by facilitating mutual awareness, a sensitive appreciation of the aspiration of the 'other' and sufficient concern to accommodate without conflict. That, of course, is achieved far more easily when the self-esteem of individuals is sufficiently high to be able to make concessions to others without fear of losing prestige, status or significance.

The fostering of personal relationships, the effective and just resolution of conflict, the facilitation of mutual awareness and empathy, the diminution of authoritarian systems which perpetuate alienation and distance between various members of a particular community or organization are truly Christian objectives which can be put into operation whenever a Christian unit exists. The Church must be seen to be providing answers to the anonymity and impersonality of modern society and this has to become one of its principal concerns in the future.

These principles can be fostered at home in encouraging new relationships between the sexes, between parents and their children, teachers and pupils, priests and parishioners, bishops and their dioceses, Christians in industry and the professions acting as the leaders for reducing the impersonality of modern society. They must become the guiding issues for Christian leaders so that the Church is seen to be taking a hand in the theory and practice of saving the world from the heresy of material progress, which ignores the personal significance of our neighbour created in the love which reflects the image of God.

NOTES

56   DOMINIAN, J. (1972) *The Way* (12, 3), p.199
57   DOMINIAN, J. (1975) *The Clergy Review* (60, 3), p.151
58   DOMINIAN, J. (Spring 1975) *The Ampleforth Journal* (Vol.80), p.10
59   DOMINIAN, J. (1975) *Cycles of Affirmation* (London, Darton, Longman & Todd), p.81.

The authority of Christ

The thesis presented in the last two chapters has been twofold. Firstly, the bonds which held society together in the pre-industrial period were primarily intimate ones linked with the family and the fact that those responsible for production and consumption of essential goods were also in close proximity to each other, whereas the advent of industrialization and urbanization has progressively severed these bonds, increasing anonymity and impersonality. Secondly, the ensuing lack of cohesion was camouflaged by authoritarian structures which remained widespread in industry, business, the professions and in society in general. These were extensions of parent—child dependence patterns of the early years of childhood, translated in adult life into terms of economic, emotional and social dependence backed by sanctions of fear, awe and guilt.

Christianity has participated in this social evolution, and has, in my opinion, singularly failed to promote the principles of the kingdom of God, which have Christ and love as their centre, but has relied on the same authoritarian structures as the rest of society to underpin the propaganda of the Good News. This has been an error of major dimensions, so that in our century, when these authoritarian structures are being increasingly attacked and altered, the faith of Christians has been severely undermined in so far as it has rested on the shifting sands of authority and not on the rock of Christ himself.

I cannot claim the knowledge of a theologian and so what follows is the commentary of a psychiatrist on his understanding of the concept of authority in Christ and, as a psychiatrist, I shall use the texts of the scriptures in the way which I believe they were first written, namely as a response of inspired writers to the reality of first-hand or subsequent experience of Jesus. The scriptures are for me first and foremost psychological documents of an interpersonal encounter between the Lord and his apostles, whatever allowances may be required for social, anthropological, historical, linguistic and other reasons.

Something which has existed since the beginning,
that we have heard,
that we have seen with our own eyes;
that we have watched
and touched with our hands
the Word, who is life
this is our subject.

1 John 1:1

Christ's first experience of authority was like any other human being's, that of his relationship with his parents and I have described some aspects of this in two articles.[60], [61] I have argued there that, although Christ lived under the authority of his parents, by the age of twelve he had managed to achieve a sufficient degree of separation from them to know that his identity was fundamentally linked in his relationship with the Father, without rejecting his earthly parents.

This relationship with his Father is the key to all his authority and it is vital to appreciate the nature of the relationship. Christ is obedient to the will of the Father.

All that the Father gives me will come to me
and whoever comes to me
I shall not turn him away,
because I have come from heaven
not to do my own will,
but to do the will of the one who sent me.

John 6: 37-38

But this is not the obedience which is consequent of the inequality, immaturity or dependence which are the characteristics on early childhood in the sense that the parents have powers which the child has not and without which it perishes physically and psychologically. There is no inequality of worth.

The Father and I are one. *John 10:30*

There is no immaturity in the sense of lacking fulness or wholeness.

I am the way, the Truth and the Life. *John 14:6*

There is no dependence in the sense that Christ lacked anything essential for being.

For the Father who is the source of life
has made the Son the source of life. *John 5:26*

Everything the Father has is mine. *John 16:15*

The relationship to the Father was one of utter equality, in the presence of differentiating roles as persons of the Trinity. But what then is the basis of the obedience if not on any characteristics of inequality? On the answer depends the whole Christian understanding of relationship, authority and obedience. Christ's relationship of obedience to the authority of his Father was based on that of love and on absolutely nothing else.

This was the love Christ knew the Father had for him, to which he responded freely and without any sense of compulsion or coercion.

> The Father loves me,
> because I lay down my life
> in order to take it up again.
> No one takes it from me;
> I lay it down of my own free will.
>
> *John 10: 17-18*

And also the love he had for the Father.

> But the world must be brought to know that I love the Father
> and that I am doing exactly what the Father told me.
>
> *John 14:31*

St John's gospel makes it very clear how intimately linked obedience and love are in Christ's life, and therefore how the Christian contribution to authority must be totally concentrated on this reality in which obedience to God is exercised in and through love, and for no other reason. What is more, the basis of this loving obedience was not a response to an extrinsic authority which had powers to compel or coerce but to the oneness between the Father and the Son. The obedience of love from Son to Father is often portrayed theologically as the symbol of absolute obedience required and owed to God. In my view that is a mistaken theological concept. The obedience in fact arises out of the certainty of the relationship of love which the unity of Father and Son established. It is not obedience to an external source of power but obedience to the source of all love which Christ knew in the fulness of his being and which, John's Gospel tries to make absolutely clear, is Christ's invocation of our own obedience to God. Christ wants us to love the Father as he loves him.

> May they all be one,
> Father, may they be one in us,
> as you are in me and I am in you,
> so that the world may believe it was you who sent me.
> I have given them the glory you gave to me,
> that they may be one as we are one.

With me in them and you in me,
may they be so completely one
that the world will realize that it was you who sent me
and that I have loved them as much as you loved me.

John 17: 21-23

Father, the hour has come:
glorify your Son,
so that your Son may glorify you;
And, through the power over all mankind that you have given him,
let him give eternal life to all those you have entrusted to him.
And eternal life is this:
to know you,
the only true God.
and Jesus Christ whom you have sent.

John 17:1-3

The kingdom of God is about eternal life and eternal life is, according to John, concerned with the acknowledgment of Jesus Christ, and through him the Father, through the sharing of the bond of love which is the foundation of Christ's relationship to the Father. In my view this is the principal meaning of authority in Christianity, which is to be found in an ever-deepening understanding of the meaning of love. Christ gave a new commandment to his apostles to love one another:

I give you a new commandment,
love one another;
just as I have loved you,
you also must love one another.
By this love you have for one another
everyone will know you are my disciples.

John 13:34-35

This new commandment had the ultimate meaning for Christ because John reveals to us in his first epistle that 'God is love' (John 4:8). Therefore the ultimate authority of God rests in love. The manifestation of the divine authority in Christ not only reflected his relationship of love with his Father but also his ability to convey the meaning of love in his own life and in the quality of life appropriate for the kingdom of God which commenced here and now in this world.

There can be no doubt that Christ made a deep impression on those around him because — 'He taught them with authority and not like their own scribes' *(mt. 7:29)*.

But how was this authority revealed in and through love? In a life of love which reflected his authority and stamped it with very clear characteristics. The authority of love or the love in his authority is to be manifested first and foremost in service: 'You know that among the pagans their so-called rulers lord it over them, and their great men make their authority felt. This is not to happen among you. No; anyone who wants to become great among you must be your servant, and anyone who wants to be first amongst you must be slave to all. For the Son of Man himself, did not come to be served but to serve, and to give his life as a ransom for many.' *(Mk. 10:42-45)*.

Service is the key to authority. But service means personal availability, and the authority of Christ, as indeed of every Christian, is to be identified in the rendering of service which makes the self available to others. It is here, of course, in this availability of the self, that a hundred years of psychological insights have made some of the greatest contributions to our understanding of man. Traditionally service and availability have been understood in terms of man's sinfulness, which limits both. That sinfulness has been described as selfishness, egoism, self-centredness, greed, avarice, lust, but these terms no longer do justice to the growing and clearer psychological understanding of the unfolding of the human personality and it is in the depths of psychology that so much of the mystery of the image of God in man will be found. But that image of God is to be found fully in Christ so that, by describing some of the main findings of psychology and relating them to our understanding of Christ, we have a vital and precious key to understanding the nature of love and comprehending the mystery of God more clearly.

Personal availability is dependent on wholeness. We cannot give to others what we do not possess ourselves. Thus availability depends on the greatest possible development of our own wholeness. Man is a unity of his physical, psychological (intellectual and emotional dimensions), social and spiritual realities. Our wholeness depends on the greatest possible harmonious realization of the conscious and unconscious potential of these realities.

The realization of this potential next depends on our self-esteem, on the affirmative acceptance of ourselves. There is no point in having the most powerful body or mind, the greatest social aptitude if we *feel* insignificant, helpless, bad, inadequate or unworthy. If we do not feel good, we nullify whatever objective goodness and talent we own. An affirmative acceptance of ourselves is essential if we are to be available to others and, if it is truly affirmative, if we really feel good and secure in our own reality, then we are much more likely to act out the Christian commandment of loving our neighbour as ourselves. We love ourselves through self-acceptance. We love others through making ourselves available to them. The relationship of these elements to Christ has been explained in two essays elsewhere.[62]

This affirmative availability to others requires however another characteristic, namely empathy. Through empathy we are able to become aware of the inner world of another person. The greater our awareness of the inner world of another person, the greater will be our ability to respond accurately to their mood, physical and emotional needs, to grasp their unexpressed yearnings, to clarify their confusion and facilitate the emergence of themselves without the intrusion of our own interpretation of reality. The difference between advice and counselling is that in the former we care but give a point of view which applies to our own life: in other words, that is how we would act, think, respond in the circumstances offered to us. In counselling we care by facilitating the appropriate response of the 'other' who acts, thinks, responds in a way that retains his independence, does not become an extension of ourselves, and therefore does justice to his own wholeness and integrity.

Christ certainly had this capacity of awareness of what was going on in others, evidence of which — as one might expect — is to be found in the most psychological of all gospels, namely that of John: 'During his stay in Jerusalem for the Passover many believed in his name when they saw the signs he gave, but Jesus knew them all and did not trust himself to them; he never needed evidence about any man; he could tell what a man had in him' *(John 2:23-25)*.

This awareness of others is enhanced if the relationship which ensues is one of equality. Authoritarian philosophy stresses the power of those who have authority and the helplessness of those who do not. This means that there is an intrinsic inequality in the status of the two. Those who have power are the givers, with the magnanimity of not needing but simply endowing. When those in authority become angry or their dignity is offended, they have to be mollified and placated. Then they are expected to show magnanimity, mercy and compassion. In relationships of equality much of this hierarchical exchange does not occur.

Instead, what matters is the fulness of love exchanged. The sorrow, distress and feelings of badness arise out of the failure to love enough. The need for reparation exists whenever our love has been less than full and the deficiency has hurt or damaged another person by a deed of commission or omission. When we are the recipients of such a failure of love, this does not constitute an attack on our dignity, status, power or significance requiring restitution for such an offence and giving us the opportunity to be merciful, magnanimous and compassionate. Instead, what is required is the ability to make it possible for the person who has hurt us to make reparation to us without losing his self-respect. It is no good pretending that we have not been hurt. We can and must acknowledge this, but the hurt is mutual. On our part we have suffered a loss of love; the other has suffered the loss of being a loving person. Our responsibility is to restore, as far as it is humanly possible, the other's capacity to love.

Christ made it abundantly clear that he related on the basis of equality and friendship:

> This is my commandment;
> love one another
> as I have loved you.
> A man can have no greater love
> than to lay down his life for his friends.
> You are my friends,
> if you do what I command you.
> I shall not call you servants any more,
> because a servant does not know
> his master's business.
> I call you friends,
> because I have made known to you
> everything I have learnt from my Father.
>
> *John 15:12-16*

The greatest expression of love is total availability to another person which ultimately can require one's life. Christ realized that that was what he had to do. But his death was only justified in the pursuit of love because in that way, through death and resurrection, he could show his divine power in contradistinction to the power of authority, which uses coercion and aggression and seeks to destroy whoever threatens it.

Some will criticize the previous sections as too idealistic. After all, in order to remain in a relationship of service and availability where love continues and prevails, it is important to handle aggression towards us. It is all very well describing love in these terms, but in an imperfect world there are always those who will criticize, attack and even attempt to destroy us. Christianity is at its weakest at this point because theory and practice of Christian life have clashed violently. Christianity is a faith of love and peace and yet the actions of Christian authority have often been identified with aggression, war and the failure to implement love and peace. Perhaps we should not be too critical over a matter which is so complex and difficult to achieve. Nevertheless, much time and thought have been spent on the theology of a just war and too little on understanding the supreme importance of the Christian message, which identifies authority with service and service with availability. There cannot be service or availability in the pursuit of love unless relationships are maintained and not severed. Christianity should not be primarily concerned with the theology of the just war but with the psychology of maintaining viable relationships — indeed, one of my definitions of love is staying in relationship.

The teaching of Christ gives us powerful answers to this problem. One essential feature in the maintenance of relationship is to avoid judgments and condemnations. Putting the blame on others is one way of preserving our self-esteem. There are people who can never admit to having done anything wrong. This is not just simply stubbornness. Their denial is often held genuinely. They cannot accept any sense of badness or criticism because their underlying feelings about themselves are already so markedly self-rejecting that a conscious admission of their badness will overwhelm their bruised, battered self-image. So all badness has to be projected on somebody else. It is always somebody else's fault. The same behaviour applies when a person is so afraid or guilty of accepting responsibility that this is denied even in the face of overwhelming evidence to the contrary. Habitual liars belong to this category of vulnerable people who cannot face the truth about themselves so blame someone else if the slightest opportunity arises.

If, on the other hand, the person's self-esteem is high, then accepting responsibility is easier because a mistake, fault or bad action will not threaten the destruction of their wholeness. Their sense of goodness is greater than their sense of badness, and so responsibility can be admitted without threatening the security of their whole being. They do not need scapegoats and have nothing to gain from the discomfort of others. They do not need the diminution of others to boost their own significance. Thus they are likely to be slow to judge or condemn others.

John puts the following words in the mouth of Christ:

> You judge by human standards;
> I judge no one.
>
> *John 8:15*

Nevertheless, it is one thing not to judge in the sense of condemnation but another not to evaluate the deeds of others. Some of these deeds are in fact judged to be bad and they may do us harm. Here is an important aspect of love, how to remain in relationship with those who have genuinely hurt us, whether consciously and deliberately or by default and unintentionally. In either case, what is needed is forgiveness. It is easier to forgive the latter than the former but forgiveness is essential if we are to stay in relationship with others. The words of

95

Christ on forgiveness are unbelievably demanding but they offer the criteria for the type of life expected in the kingdom of God: 'You have learnt how it was said: You must love your neighbour and hate your enemy. But I say this to you: love your enemies and pray for those who persecute you; in this way you will be sons of your Father in heaven for he causes his sun to rise on bad men as well as good, and his rain to fall on honest and dishonest men alike. For if you love those who love you, what right have you to claim any credit? Even the tax collectors do as much, do they not? And if you save your greetings for your brothers, are you doing anything exceptional? Even the pagans do as much, do they not? You must therefore be perfect just as your heavenly Father is perfect'. *(Mt 5:43-48)*.

And this loving of one's enemy requires forgiveness, which is described by Matthew: 'Then Peter went up to him and said, "Lord, how often must I forgive my brother if he wrongs me? As often as seven times?" Jesus answered, "Not seven, I tell you, but seventy-seven times" ' *(Mt 18:21-22)*.

Thus a non-judgmental attitude combined with forgiveness are the criteria by which relationships can and should be maintained if love is to be present. As already suggested, both of these are infinitely easier to achieve when the relationship is one of equality and the esteem of those concerned high, which avoids the need to save face.

The aim of staying in relationship is not a static one. By remaining in relationship with one another the conditions are present for the promotion of sustaining, healing and mutual growth,[63] and authority as service has the responsibility to ensure that these three essential human characteristics are achieved in any community where there are relationships which are not purely temporary and transient in nature.

The ultimate of availability as an expression of service is the giving up of one's life for the sake of another. Christ did that on the cross and, before his death, made himself personally available in the Eucharist. But we can only die physically once, whereas we can die for each other many times in and through love. This is the death which offers part or the whole of ourselves to others in physical, emotional or social sacrifice. The effectiveness of authority as service is to be seen in that combination which ensures that the life of the person in authority approximates as closely as possible to that of Christ and the fruits of that person's authority act as a catalyst to promote love in the community for which he is responsible.

Such a view is a rejection of authority which primarily relies on and uses power. When Christ finally acknowledged his kingship before Pilate he also proclaimed the value system of the kingdom which he came to proclaim and live: 'So Pilate went back into the Praetorium and called Jesus to him. "Are you the King of the Jews?" he asked. Jesus replied — "Do you ask this of your own accord, or have others spoken to you about me?" Pilate answered, "Am I a Jew? It is your own people and the chief priests who have handed you over to me: what have you done?" Jesus replied — "Mine is not a kingdom of this world; if my kingdom were of this world, my men would have fought to prevent my being surrendered to the Jews. But my kingdom is not of this kind." "So you are a king then?" said Pilate. "It is you who say it" answered Jesus. "Yes, I am a king. I was born for this; I came into this world for this: to bear witness to the truth and all who are on the side of faith listen to my voice".' *(John 18:33-38)*.

But the kingdom of God does not require a register of legitimate and just authority for the running of society. There are passages in Paul's[64] and Peter's epistles[65] which stress the importance of obeying legitimate authority to the full and, indeed, it could not be otherwise for no society could hope to have the conditions for the promotion of the kingdom of God that did not have a semblance of order, justice, peace (which need support from the civil authority). But the Christian must go beyond that to act as the salt of the earth, the leaven; to promote the fulness of being which is the kingdom. Here authority has an entirely different purpose: to act as a reminder to secular authority that beyond order, justice and peace the objectives of love are to be sought, which can only be promoted by the concept of authority as service, which in turn means personal availability for the sake of sustaining, healing and growth which Christ gave us as his credentials of authority.

NOTES

60   DOMINIAN, J. (1975) "Human and Divine Love" in *Cycles of Affirmation* (London, Darton, Longman & Todd), p. 2
61   DOMINIAN, J. (1975) "The Relationship between Christ and Mary" in *The Way* (Supp.25), p.58
62   DOMINIAN, J. (1975) "Integrity of Person" I and II, in *Cycles of Affirmation* (London, Darton, Longman & Todd), pp. 28, 36
63   DOMINIAN, J. (1975) "The Cycle of Human Affirmation" in *Cycles of Affirmation* (London, Darton, Longman & Todd), p.152
64   Romans 13: 1—7
65   1 Peter 2:13

Education for authority

I

The changing attitude towards authority has placed a considerable strain on all educators, parents, teachers and leaders, in all walks of life, who have the responsibility of caring for others. The debate is usually polarized in such simple terms as 'too much or too little discipline'.

Since children and men and women of all ages can be coerced through varieties of fear to behave in a way that appears cohesive, orderly and efficient, those who advocate strictness can find champions in all societies and in all social groups to support their view. Fear is a powerful shaper of human behaviour. It has also the backing of the fact that some of our most powerful earliest experiences were based on inequalities that made fear an effective intervening element in behaviour even though it was not overtly exercised as such. A young baby arrives in the world and for some years remains bound by inequalities between itself and others: inequalities of size, capacity and the need for approval.

Man is born in a state of dependence, and fear of the loss of support of others is an intrinsic element in our survival. The dependence on others in early childhood is that of physical, emotional and economic care, and those needs remain to a greater or lesser extent throughout our life. Since one essential characteristic of negotiating our dependence is obedience towards those who meet our needs, obedience has come to be regarded as the crucial characteristic for the effective functioning of society. For believers it has become the key element in their response to God. Such a view is very understandable, but it is naive and a gross violation of human integrity.

Although we are born in a state of dependence, the meaning of life is to be found not in dependence but in relationship. The key to order, effectiveness and love lies in that more complex reality of relationship within which obedience plays an important but subordinate role.

The world is engaged at all levels in a gigantic reappraisal of this change in direction from a simplistic order of authority seen as power related to obedience to one of relationship between states, within individual societies and within family units in which interaction is based on free choice and an equality of worth in the presence of differentiating characteristics. This revaluation of the meaning of life is linked to the complex but very important term 'human dignity'. Until now I have examined that universal reappraisal primarily in psychological terms. Of course there are other dimensions of social, economic, political and legal significance in which authority, power, compliance and sanctions apply, but all would agree that the way we are educated has a decisive influence on our attitudes towards authority. Therefore I shall conclude with a psychological study of education for authority.

II

Psychology can help us to further human potential by examining the unfolding physical, emotional, intellectual and social resources of the child. It can help us to ensure that the response of authority is one of service and not of power: service dedicated to the facilitation of the intrinsic potential of the child.

A child's potential is to be found in its inherited characteristics, modified in the course of its nine months in the womb. After birth these characteristics are facilitated or inhibited by the attitude of all those who surround the child and are responsible for its education. This is called the impact of nurture and our ultimate human potential is a compound of nature and nurture. Nurture plays a vital role in our attitude to human relationships and the following factors are crucial in this development.

The first factor is the attitude of the parents towards their child. As originators of a particular life they can see themselves as its proprietors and adopt an attitude of having proprietary rights as absolute sources of its origin. Therefore they either see the child as an inevitably dependent extension of themselves, or consider the new life as a free, absolute gift to its owner with only one consequent possibility: a free relationship thereafter. The view the parents adopt of themselves or of God as creator is fundamental to the interpretation of the meaning of authority. If the second orientation is adopted, then the parents, who are the source of a new life, accept the responsibility of service. That will ensure that the child realizes its potential for entering into full, free relationships of equality with them and with others. Any other attitude inevitably sees the source of life as a source of power and that determines the quality of the exchange thereafter. In this book I have assumed that the source of life, whether God or parents, donates a free gift to the recipient. They do this out of love and seek in return a relationship of love which can only be fulfilled when the new life is encouraged and equipped with the capacity of love.

If these premisses are accepted then the source of life is not an authority invested with power, but a source of responsible service whose main task is the promotion of the independence and realized potential of the child.

All growth of the child is a process of gradual separation between itself and the parents; a gradual loss of its dependence on them; and the mobilization of its resources. The reduction of dependence occurs continuously, but has certain peak periods in which autonomy manifests itself in a more acute form. There are three such peak periods. The first is in the second and third year of life in which the child acquires an extensive new range of abilities. Standing up, crawling, walking, talking, feeding, dressing itself, handling objects, learning to play, all occur round this period and the parents' attitude is crucial.

1. The child's first efforts at autonomy are clumsy, messy and time-consuming. If the parents see themselves as facilitators they have to accept the time and responsibility for allowing the trial-and-error experimentation of young children. Most parents accept this but some take over and begin to take the first step of handicapping the child by doing things for it, so that dependence is prolonged and possibly accentuated.

2. As autonomy extends beyond the household into the world outside, in the house of a neighbour, in the street (provided it is safe), in the nursery school, another hindering element enters in: parental anxiety or rigidity. The first hindrance by parents is their tendency to take over; the second is the curtailing of independent action outside the home (and sometimes inside it) because of anxiety about damage or injury. These hindrances can continue throughout childhood but begin to be seen in this early stage of education.

3. Most important of all, is the quality of experience the child receives at the hands of its parents. If the parents recognize the life of their child as a gift freely donated by them, then all its achievements will be affirmed and confirmed as part of the build up of its self-esteem. Its achievements are not meant to be an extension of the parent's power. They belong to the child and form part of its own intrinsic goodness which gradually will become the coffers of its own treasury, and will enable it to relate to others. Naturally in this early stage of growth the intimacy of child and parent is so close that all the child's achievements are heavily related to the feelings it has towards its mother and father, and its motivation will be to please them. This desire to please the parents and yet at the same time gain autonomy is one of the crucial features of the human drama of growth and infinitely

more important than Freud's resolution of the oedipal complex. Every step towards autonomy is potentially a conflict situation with parents who might say 'No', or 'Don't do that', with an act of rebellion as the result. Rebellion is a strong word to use of this early stage in life, but the pursuit of the child's objective in defiance of parental wishes produces a recurrent conflict situation beloved of authoritarian figures. Is the child allowed to do what it wants? Should the parent be entirely permissive? These and similar questions are fired at anyone who attacks the sacrosanct nature of authority conceived as power.

The answers are clear and precise. Of course the child needs to learn that it cannot pursue its own wishes in an unrestrained manner. At this early stage of development it is not open to reason, logic or argument. Control is undoubtedly an exhibition of power. The verbal No, the slight tap, the smack will all be used. That is to assume that the parents have in turn been responsible and ensured that precious objects are not within reach and in danger of being broken; that doors are not left open which allow the possibility of dangerous wandering; that they behave consistently and with restraint in their own actions; that demands are reasonable and within the capacity of the child rather than expecting the understanding of an adult; and that they show patience. In this pre-school period the means of control are almost invariably aversive, that is to say there is a simple conditioning effect by which the child learns approval or disapproval in very simple terms. The child however is not to be treated as bad, needing punishment; it is incapable of being bad and punishment is irrelevant. What it needs and what is essential is assistance with self-control, integration of its functioning, direction, purpose — requirements which will be needed throughout childhood. But there is a world of difference between parents who conceive themselves as authority needing to correct the badness of the child and the parent-child relationship which is concerned with growth, needing assistance, shaping and directing. Now the child recognizes itself increasingly as good and lovable but nevertheless needing help. The issue is not primarily one of discipline but of giving help without depriving the child of its self-esteem. The key element in this phase is that no sense of badness is associated with the first efforts at independence, and that autonomy is not seen as a threat to the approval and love needed so urgently from the parents.

The inevitable moments of conflict introduce the experience of ambivalence, which is a technical term for the capacity to love and hate or feel love and be angry with the same person, a universal experience of mankind. This feeling starts in this first phase of autonomy because for a moment the forbidding, prohibiting, denying parent, who may also have inflicted pain either by withdrawal of love or by physical contact, is a hated object. But this feeling cannot last for long. The need to be approved, comforted and loved is too great. The capacity for a quick reconciliation without loss of status is vital to the child. If parents do not see themselves as authoritarian figures, reconciliation is not concerned with a restitution of their rights or with reparation. Nor is reconciliation a matter of authority showing mercy or benevolence. Authority as service loves the child unconditionally but acknowledges that there is a responsibility to equip it with the skills it does not possess and that this requires training. A child is not endowed with guilt feelings for having attacked the goodness or the power of parents, and reparation is not a restoration of the dignity associated with the power of parents. There is enough inevitable pain in any time, long or short, in which a child feels cut off from the source of all love. That pain is sufficiently prohibitive without any additional infliction of a sense of badness, guilt and the need of punishment.

III

The second stage of autonomy comes towards the end of the primary school period, some time between the years of eight and twelve. These are the years in which Piaget describes the child's marked shift of awareness of parents as a source of absolute power and authority, towards the presence and significance of people with whom rules and regulations can be negotiated with a reciprocal awareness of each other's existence, rights and the consequent need for the appropriate justice. By now the child has travelled a long way on the road to independence and lives already in two environments: home and school. The main attitudes towards authority continue. The parents remain the crucial figures whose approval and support are vital. But the child's resources have expanded. There is an increasing capacity to cope with aloneness and a consequent diminution of the fear of isolation. The need to be affirmed remains as strong as ever and the build up of self-esteem proceeds all the time through the continuous association of its creative achievements with a sense of goodness. Essential as this is there is another component of self-esteem which is even more important, namely the feeling of being lovable, independent of achievement. The sense of unconditional love which depends on nothing except the free gift of acceptance and affirmation offered by the parents to the child is essential for the development of the feeling of personal worth independent of actual achievements.

There are so many people who grow up in our highly competitive society feeling that their worth is dependent entirely on what they can achieve, and even more important how well that achievement pleases authority. Such people live by kind permission of others and are frequently on the brink of emotional disaster if they feel their achievements are not good enough (and they rarely feel that they are), or that authority will disapprove of them. There has to be a core of self-acceptance which gives a continuous sense of goodness without having to earn this approval anew. There are millions of men and women who feel wanted only if they can get, or give another human being money, sex or some service and, in the depths of their being, never feel loved for themselves but for what they can achieve or give. Their anxiety grows with the passage of time, with fading looks, and with impaired capacities. They dread the moment of utter rejection when they are not good enough to earn the essential measures of approval.

Parents are crucial figures in creating an image of unconditional acceptance in their children which gives the latter the feeling that they matter because they have life, they exist, they are persons, before they receive recognition on the basis of their competence or their value in competition with others. Such personal worth increasingly gives them a sense of trust, meaning and personal significance which can stand the erosion of disappointments, failures and limitations. They experience themselves as essentially good and the core of their being is good whatever limitations may surround it. This does not mean that unconditional acceptance is an excuse for indifference, neglect or failure to make use of the fullest possible potential they possess. But they are much more likely to do that with the confidence that they will not be judged on their achievements or whether they have pleased authority.

IV

But authority intrudes more and more in a new capacity: namely the structure of society, of school and of the world outside the home. Here is the beginning of that wider community which forms social structures outside the home which are based much less on the intimacy and bonds of family relationships. There are rules and regulations in every home but they are linked to close affectionate ties. There are more rules and regulations in the primary school which relate to the social effectiveness of an organization primarily concerned with . . . What is the primary school concerned with? The authoritarian personality has no doubt about the answer. The primary school is there to teach the three Rs. In an article [66] I suggested that in addition to these three Rs the school has an even greater responsibility of teaching the fourth R, which stands for relationship. The argument often proceeds from here as if the two aims were incompatible. A child can have its cognitive abilities fostered and at the same time live in a school environment where teachers, as authority figures, continue the task of seeing

103

authority as service. Their bond with the children is less intimate than that of the parents but it is still a very close one and they can structure an atmoshpere of facilitation or one of power which imparts knowledge to passive creatures waiting to soak it up. Most of the middle-aged and elderly in our society will remember that kind of education in their school, when they went there to learn facts, mostly in a passive manner. Education in primary school has come a long way from such rigidity for the school visualized as a community in which the child experiences an extension of facilitating figures to enrich its awareness of relationship as well as acquiring the necessary creative talent for those years, is the aim of the primary school. In the last year or two of the primary school, teachers will notice that decisions shift from parents as sources of absolute and unchangeable value systems, to peers; and that relationships of equality grow. Both they and the parents will become targets of this next stage of 'rebellion' and they can either see this development as something to suppress or as something to encourage.

The encouragement of the changing relationship between child and parent, child and teacher need not be, indeed must not be, at the expense of the breakdown of law and order in the school. In the primary school the child learns the need for order as a way of safeguarding the interests of other children. The concepts of co-operation, fairness and justice are now rapidly growing and it is becoming easier to see that order is required if everyone's good is to be ensured. The needs of others are increasingly recognized and respected. Others must have their turn with food, games, praise, attention and, for that to happen, there is a need for rules, regulations, order and sanctions. The primary school is a social organization in which the public good is recognized for the first time. By the eleventh and twelfth year the child has not only a concept of the public good but the beginnings of evaluating legitimacy and the way in which authority exercises its functions. Authority is now no longer absolute and increasingly there will be a critical appraisal of its functions as the capacities of the child begin to approach those of the adult.

V

Entry to the secondary school often coincides with the arrival of puberty and the beginning of adolescence. It is a phase which culminates in the third and final period of autonomy when the young man or woman becomes capable of leaving home, starting work or further education and forming sexual relationships. Up to now the young person has been expanding his physical, intellectual and social skills and, if authority has functioned as a service, the result is the feeling of increasing possession of self in an integrated and affirmative manner. The integration means that the growth of the various parameters has been congruent and the affirmation has led to a sense of being at home with one's own functions and achievements and feeling they belong to oneself. Temporarily this sense of independent existence is subjected to strain when the body is invaded with the appropriate sexual hormones and puberty is ushered in. This is physical development with several psychological consequences. Puberty adds a powerful barrier of separation between child and parent, the incest barrier. Freud saw the earliest phase of this around about the fourth or fifth year and the resolution of the oedipus complex as the most significant psychological part of the child's growth. Be that as it may, puberty allows the young girl or man the capacity of a separate sexual existence. By now the growing person is acquiring a degree of freedom to think in abstract and universal terms, to function as a separate sexual being, and is rapidly approaching the point of equality of physical and psychological functioning with adults, even though there is still a marked inequality of experience and emotional maturity.

In the secondary school young people take a further step in acquainting themselves with a duality of seeing authority as a source of service and recognizing that the social order of the school community requires rules and regulations implemented by those in charge if it is to function for the good of all. The increasing competence of the young man or woman should receive final encouragement from figures of authority, parents and teachers, so that young people are seen as guardians of the development of their potential, and in order to allow increasing co-operation and interaction on a basis of equality but of different functions. The increasing equality means that the young man or woman will be given the final offer of service from figures of authority: encouragement to allow an evaluation of this service. The evaluation will certainly be incomplete and at times incorrect but the judgment will improve and will finally leave the young person qualified to assess authority with love but critically, so that the ever-present danger of the misuse of the function of authority as a source of power is minimized.

VI

The ultimate aim of education for authority is for parents and teachers to encourage the continuous process of separation, reducing dependence continuously and furthering the growth of a person who is able to realize his potential, accept himself, feel lovable for his significance independently of his achievements, rejoice in his achievements but be conscious of his defects and, from the depths of such affirmation, evaluate authority in a way that differentiates and discriminates its use as an instrument of coercive power rather than service. If education has been positive, it becomes a model of service for the growing person who in turn will offer to his children and to others what he has learned.

Because people felt trusted, they know the meaning of trust and can offer it to others. Because they felt accepted, they know the meaning of acceptance and they can offer it to others. Because they received more love than rejection, they love more than they reject, and finally they can see the good in others more than they see the badness. Because their independence has been acknowledged they know the meaning of freedom, can offer it and respect it in others. Because their equality has been recognized they feel their value independently of their achievements or capacities and they can trust others with the same motivation of equality, of worth independent of talents. Because they feel good, confident and secure, they are not easily susceptible to corruption, fear or coercion and they have no need to acquire a false sense of goodness, confidence or security by mastering, dominating, humiliating or conquering others. Such men and women have an inner freedom which they instinctively want to respect in others, and wish indeed to do all they can to bring it about in others.

Authority as service is responsible for such achievement. Authoritarian figures who see authority as a pyramid of power produce the opposite characteristics either in personal relationships or in the societies they control. They are concerned with managing and controlling others, fearful that if they lose control others will control them. In controlling others fear plays a large part. Sanctions and punishment predominate and so does a sense of badness. A sense of badness cripples the capacity to give or to receive love in close relationships. The sense of badness creates indifference, contempt, corruption and disregard of the value of others, whose only value is seen as a stepping-stone for the promotion of one's own advantage. Economic, social and political corruption exist when the 'other' is an expendable unit present to support the inner impoverishment of individuals or a group that has little sense of its own value except at the expense of others.

All the characteristics described in this chapter belong to humanity as a whole. There is no concept of two cities in this book. The kingdom of God is not an entity separate from this world as we know it. There are not two sets of standards. All that has been written applies to every human being, even though different social structures will realize different aspects of what has been described. The kingdom of God as revealed in the Old and the New Testaments is unfolded in the living tradition of the Christian community and the truth present in all authentic religion is not a reality separate from the secular world.

The kingdom of God is the image of God unfolding in man as humanity explores the mystery of life in an ever-deepening understanding and grasp of its manifold dimensions. This century's preoccupation with a revaluation of authority is fundamental to the kingdom of God and, as shown in the previous two chapters, there is nothing in the authentic pursuit of this subject which is inconsistent with revelation and the life of Christ.

The fundamental pursuit of the age is equality of worth in terms of social justice and personal relationships. That is at the heart of the Christian message, and the most urgent responsibility of the Christian community is to remove authoritarian systems and structures as the language and medium of expressing the Good News. The massive withdrawal from Christianity is largely due to the basic anachronism in all Christian denominations, for they have all ignored the message of equality and love pursued by the world. The world is right; its aspirations are wholly consistent with Jesus's message to the world; but to implement those aspirations it needs the Good News and the suffering, death and resurrection of Jesus. A world that seeks the truth intuitively but lacks the support of Christ is a confused world. When the Christian community assumes the role of authority as service and in that way brings Jesus back into the life of the people, the legitimate aspirations of humanity can go forward on the way to the realization of the kingdom of God.

NOTES

66   DOMINIAN, J. (November 1974) *Teachers World* (No. 3393)